FUGITIVES OF INCEST
A Perspective from
Psychoanalysis and Groups

FUGITIVES OF INCEST
A Perspective from Psychoanalysis and Groups

Ramon C. Ganzarain, M.D. and
Bonnie J. Buchele, Ph.D.

International Universities Press
Madison, Connecticut

Copyright © 1988, Ramon C. Ganzarain and Bonnie J. Buchele,

Library of Congress Cataloging-in-Publication Data

Ganzarain, Ramon C.
  Fugitives of incest: a perspective from psychoanalysis and groups
/ Ramon C. Ganzarain and Bonnie J. Buchele.
    p. cm.
  Bibliography: p.
  Includes index.
  ISBN 0-8236-2102-2
  1. Incest. 2. Group psychoanalysis. I. Buchele, Bonnie Jean
Cadwalader. II. Title.
RC560.I53G36 1988   88-3639
616.85'83—dc 19   CIP

Manufactured in the United States of America

To our patients for teaching us,
to our families for encouraging us,
and to our colleagues for helping us

Contents

Preface

The secretive nature of consummated incest seems to pervade the mental health professional's attitude toward the subject: the attention devoted to it has fallen far short of its importance. It is as if for a long time the taboo against consummated incest has been extended to any discussion of the subject. More recently, however, incest has become a timely topic and is now discussed more openly. But even now discourse is focused largely on description, direct intervention to protect children, and prevention. By contrast, this book deals with the treatment of adults who as children were victims of incest.

Incest is difficult to define, two sources of confusion being the many varieties of sexual activities and the numerous types of kinship between victims and perpetrators. For instance, some authors (Henderson, 1975) focus on "intimate physical contact accompanied by conscious sexual excitement" between incestuous partners, but a whole variety of voyeuristic/exhibitionistic sexual interactions are excluded by this definition. Likewise, incestuous partners are often defined as close blood relatives, but this omits adoptive, in-law, and step relationships as well as other bonds that develop within the context of a shared socialization unit. Generally people do not think of incest as possible between members of the same sex, as is reflected for instance in British law; in England the legal definition of incest excludes homosexual activities (Ciba Foundation, 1984).

Part of the difficulty in defining incest is that different cultures have different ideas as to what sexual bonds are forbidden. Within the royal families of ancient Egypt, Greece, Peru, and Japan, some forms of incest were condoned. Contemporary Japanese psychiatrists (Takahashi, 1986, personal communication) state that mother-son incest seems the most frequent variety; in Western cultures, by contrast, father-daughter and sibling incest predominate.

Sigmund Freud (Breuer and Freud, 1893–1895) dominates the early psychiatric literature on psychotherapy for the consequences of incest. He acknowledged the existence of child sexual abuse and developed the traumatic or "seduction" theory of neurosis. However, when he discovered psychic reality, or unconscious fantasy, as a cause of mental conflicts and symptoms, he deemphasized the relative pathogenic importance of trauma. In recent decades, the confluence of the child protection and feminist movements has focused attention on incest once again. Freud's theories have often been misunderstood as if he discounted the actual occurrence of intrafamilial sexual abuse and its effects (Herman and Hirschman, 1977; Masson, 1982; Ciba Foundation, 1984). The controversy has been inflamed by the fact that incest is a secret crime that has both a victim and a perpetrator, whose abuse can have serious legal ramifications including possible destruction of the family and the abuser's incarceration.

Incest is much more prevalent than was at first believed. Exact figures are unavailable because this crime often goes unreported and legal definitions vary according to jurisdiction. Summitt (1983) estimates that 10 percent of American women are sexually abused by relatives, while Russell (1986) found a 16 percent rate. The extent of incestuous abuse of male children is relatively unknown. The reporting by boys seems to decrease with age.

Perusal of the recent literature on incest reveals that diagnosis and treatment of adults incestuously abused in childhood is seldom discussed (Henderson, 1975; Lystad, 1982; Vander Mey and Neff, 1982). Until recently, little was known about the specific dynamics of the serious familial dysfunctions that accompany incest, or about the symptoms now seen as characteristic of adults who as children were incest victims. Gelinas (1983) filled part of this gap by describing the atmosphere of the incestuous family; she includes a constellation of behaviors that may guide the clinician in determining the presence of intrafamilial sexual abuse. Ellenson (1986) describes diagnostic elements—perceptual distortions, memories, dissociative phenomena—which when present are positive indications of consummated incest.

A great many patients in long-term treatment, patients who initially present themselves with problems other than incest victimization, will in time disclose a history of incest that later may become the central clinical issue. Few of these cases, however, make their way into the literature. Some analysts have reported the psychoanalysis of individual cases (Rascovsky and Rascovsky, 1950; Kramer, 1983), while a few group psychotherapists have written of their experiences treating adult victims, but using a relatively short-term approach (Herman and Hirschman, 1977; Knittle and Tuana, 1980; Herman and Schatzow, 1984; Blake-White and Kline, 1985; Cole, 1985; Deighton and McPeek, 1985).

By contrast, this book describes our experience with long-term psychoanalytically oriented group psychotherapy of persons with an early history of incest. We invite our patients to attend the group for a minimum of one year and convey to them the following goals: to work through trauma, to overcome the resultant conflicts, and to achieve a better integration of their personalities. Our work as cotherapists was organized in a collaborative way as follows. We jointly dictated notes about each group session, discussing them together; we planned strategies dealing with future interventions, referrals, consultations, and so on. We discussed our feelings and differences privately with each other, but without sharing them with the patients. During sessions we do not usually exchange verbal comments with one another.

For this population group psychotherapy offers several advantages. First is the provision of a peer group offering several transferential targets, thereby decreasing the likelihood of an intense, chaotic transference. Second, countertransference emotions are tempered by the presence of group members, who can share the affective burden of responding to emotionally laden group situations. Third, the presence of therapists of both sexes offers a surrogate "parental couple." Finally, the group-as-a-whole gives members a good-enough mothering atmosphere in which it is safe to be oneself.

To form such a group we first invited individual psychotherapists to refer to us their adult patients (eighteen years or older) who were presently in treatment and had a clear history of incest victimization. The idea was to offer these patients concurrent individual and group psychotherapy. The two of us met regularly and during crises with individual psychotherapists, probation officers, hospital staff, and marital, family, and sex therapists. Our goal was to integrate all aspects of each patient's treatment. We started our group in February 1984, having selected seven members from the first thirteen referrals. These seven included one man, but he dropped out before the first group meeting. Before that meeting, we met with the members individually to prepare them to enter the group and to assess motivation and severity of psychopathology. Since then the group has been meeting once a week for an hour and twenty minutes. The flow of new referrals has been steady, some patients have been discharged from the group, and some have been added.

The generalizability of our findings is limited by the fact that our sample does not represent the entire population of incest victims. Since all referrals had experienced significant emotional problems in their daily functioning, the sample did not include persons who can satisfactorily cope with their lives. Persons who were amnestic for the incest trauma were also excluded, as having clear memories of the incest was a prerequisite for entering treatment. The size of the sample is obviously small; twenty-five patients participated in a two-and-a-half-year rotation in the group, and fifty were interviewed in a variety of clinical situations. Although trends and tendencies are clearly observable, we must remain cautious until greater numbers become available.

Confidentiality is an important concern in treating these patients particularly because of their loaded, shameful secret. However, since multiple treatment modalities were required to help them, we obtained permission from the outset to discuss their cases with other treaters. In this book, their identities are of course disguised for reasons of confidentiality.

Although evaluating therapeutic outcome is not the purpose of this book, general observations are made regarding patients' progress. Since recovery from the severe trauma of incest is a lifelong process, improvement must necessarily be relative and limited. Our patients learned to express anger more directly and blamed themselves considerably less; depression was lifted, and they began to assert themselves appropriately. Some developed better marital relationships. Several resumed adult education while others learned to take considerably better care of their health. A few became more comfortable spending money on themselves. These changes are expressions of their improved self-images. Most reviewed and altered their initial perceptions of their abusers.

The deep analytic exploration of the unconscious, reached through free association, may be assumed to be unavailable in groups. But compared to psychoanalysis as a possible treatment for the emotional scars of incest, group psychotherapy has the advantage of treating a number of patients simultaneously, offering them a peer group with whom to relate, and allowing clinicians to accumulate experience with a variety of cases. The trade-off seems to be depth versus extension; however, when a group becomes cohesive, patients do explore their intimate fantasies—e.g., significant dreams are examined as a group product. Expressive group psychotherapy and psychoanalysis have in common the patients' resistances to uncovering their traumatic memories and conflicting, frustrated wishes. There is a collective therapeutic alliance in groups which overcomes such resistances. Peer example, cohesive concerns, and a regressive pull from the group facilitate the difficult integrative tasks of psychotherapy.

Immediately upon starting our group, we were forced to cope with the problems of countertransference. Time and again we found ourselves deskilled by intense emotional responses of disbelief, revulsion, and rage, by rescue fantasies, and by feelings of sexual attraction and consequent defensive reactions. Making constructive use of such feelings became central to our work. We therefore tried to study them systematically. Chapter 1 is the product of this study.

Transference reactions, as might be expected, were intense and intractable. Possible explanations for their durability include intensely negative maternal transference at the preoedipal level (often disguised as pure hatred of the abuser); early deprivations of maternal care; violent sibling rivalries and jealousy; and a defensive stance of self-sufficient omnipotence. Chapter 2 explores the topic of transference.

These patients attempted, more frequently than others, to communicate through actions a plethora of confusing feelings. As treatment progressed, acting out was frequent and dramatic. Since their ability to put concerns into words was quite limited, the main therapeutic task was to develop a willingness to explore, with the group, the meaning of such problematic actions. We deal with acting out in chapter 3.

Victims of incest are often referred to as survivors with regard to the problems they experience in developing a firm sense of self. Their self-images are often fragmented, manifesting themselves as multiple personality, false self, negative identity, and so on. This lack of integration can be worsened by major life changes. The group provides an atmosphere in which healthy attempts at renewed self-integration can take place; this is dealt with in chapter 4.

We also studied the pathogenic effects of defense mechanisms; though primarily these are intended as protection against trauma or conflict, they may secondarily induce a new set of symptoms. We reviewed alterations of ego functions such as attention, perception, memory, and consciousness and conceptualized them as expressions of post-traumatic stress disorder, mediated by the use of repression and splitting. More complex psychopathologies were viewed and studied as the consequences of defenses against several major developmental conflicts. This subject is covered in chapter 5, which also includes two detailed case studies.

We wish to acknowledge the support and helpful criticism of Mary Ann Clifft, Mahasen de Silva, Robert Dies, Virginia Eicholtz, Edoard Klain, Catherine Mayer, Mary McLin, Aleta Pennington, Claude Pigott, Jeannine Riddle, Irwin Rosen, Pearl Rosenberg, Saul Scheidlinger, William Simpson, Carol Tenpenny, Saul Tuttman, Theresa Wood, and members of the Wednesday Study Group on Groups. We are grateful also to the clinicians who referred patients to us, and to collaborating treaters.

Interest, publicity, and the availability of funds for incest studies have brought the subject out of the closet. Harm has sometimes been done by well-meaning but poorly trained helpers. Legal, educational, religious, and health professionals may be called to intervene without always having sufficient knowledge of the subject. Some helpers, given the atmosphere of urgency, may be pushed to improvise drastic actions which may be counterproductive. The resulting damage often compounds the traumatic effects of the incest. To minimize these risks, persons working with incest victims and offenders need extensive training, supervision, and a willingness to work within a multidisciplinary team approach.

   We realize that we are only beginning to learn about this
very difficult subject. Although we are now better equipped to
understand it, many new questions have arisen in the course of
our study. We hope that our own curiosity will have a stimulating
effect on that of the reader.

Chapter 1

Countertransference When Incest Is the Problem

As patients who have been victims of incest repeat within therapy the contradictory interpersonal roles learned during childhood, their therapists feel under pressure to take on roles and attitudes complementing those assumed by the patients. They feel manipulated to play a part in these patients' fantasies, a typical effect of projective identification on countertransference. In this chapter we describe several pairs of reciprocal roles, how they were assumed by the patients both in their past and in the group setting, and our countertransference responses.

Clinicians treating these patients experience intense, perplexing, and contradictory feelings: horrified disbelief, excited curiosity, sexual fantasies, related guilt, a need to blame someone, wishes to rescue. These countertransference feelings affect how one treats these patients. However, there is virtually no literature on the subject of countertransference[1] when treating

[1] In this chapter, we use countertransference to mean the whole of the therapist's unconscious and conscious attitudes and behaviors toward the patient. This broader definition goes beyond the therapist's repetition of childhood conflicts and incorporates the therapist's specific responses to the patient's personality.

1

adults sexually abused in childhood by family members. To fill this void we will report on how we as cotherapists—one female, the other male—used our emotional responses to understand these patients and to develop effective psychotherapeutic strategies in dealing with them in a group setting.

When prospective patients were offered the possibility of entering our group, most of them initially responded with a feeling of relief. They would say, "Finally I will meet people who believe me and who can really understand me," or "Now, I'll be able to talk about my awful secret with people who have gone through something comparable." However, some patients were reluctant to join the group, asking, "Will there be people in the group I know? Perhaps they are friends I have hidden from and now I'll be forced to share with them my shameful secret." A related response of shame was verbalized as: "Well, if people know that I am part of the group led by you two doctors, then everybody will know I am a victim of incest. I will be publicly labeled in the community." Adding to their reluctance was a fear that joining the group would be a disloyal act and would result in their losing their "special" status. Seven patients, all women, were initially selected for the group, which started in February 1984. They ranged in age from eighteen to forty-five, and in socioeconomic status from lower to upper class.

Reciprocal Roles

We will describe a mixture of transference patterns and social attitudes expressed as roles, and explain how these roles influence countertransference through projective identification inducing role suction (Redl, 1963) and/or role reversals.

As transferences developed in the group, patients experienced with the therapists a reenactment of their parental relations. Contradictory roles learned during childhood returned in the context of therapy. Patients sometimes shifted from one role to its opposite (e.g., from "victim" to "favorite"), thus confusing the therapists. Each role had its reciprocal. When a patient assumed one role, she put pressure on the therapists to assume its complementary opposite. We conceptualize these phenomena as the ways in which projective identification operates as a defense mechanism (Ogden, 1979; Horwitz, 1983).

Some of the roles these patients assume are familial. They fluctuate between being the parent and being the child. Incest marks The End—the end of childhood and the beginning of a pseudoadult sexual life. If the incest partner is the father or the mother, that means the child loses the abusing parent, who no longer will be available in any normal capacity. From then on these children are pushed into a parental role. They are encouraged to act as partners, sexually but also in other ways. Usually they are pushed into parenting their parents, who themselves feel inadequately parented. Many examples of this type of interaction have occurred in the group. For example, when the male therapist, whose native language is Spanish, mispronounced an English work, one member hastened, in a very maternal way, to correct his error.

At home incest victims become "favorites" through love and seduction or, just the opposite, are subjected to violence and abuse of power. Seduction is forced on them by exploiting their need for love and approval. They feel like "possessions," "pieces of property" owned by the adults who seduce them. One woman who dropped out of the group early feared other group members would criticize her love for her father and how much she enjoyed her favored status within the family. Mainly she feared being criticized for not having stopped the incest.

Sometimes clinicians feel that the adults who "victimized" these patients are to be blamed. They forget that there is an intricate and ambivalent relationship between these incestuous persons and parents, with basically a close relationship. Although angry feelings may also be present, there is a background of loyalty. Any failure by the therapist to acknowledge this paradox can place these patients in an untenable position where they feel misunderstood.

Another pair of childhood roles assumed by these individuals are those of "rival" (either of the parent of the opposite sex or of the one of the same sex) and "dependent small child" in need of protection and nurturance. For example, one patient sat in the female cotherapist's seat in her absence. The patient, feeling guilty about occupying the therapist's chair, as well as about acting as cotherapist with the male therapist, made many defensive statements denying any implications of rivalry. Two other patients abruptly left the group, like small helpless children forced to run away from home. Both felt financially exploited by their fathers, who had sexually abused them; they had left home after the fathers offered to support them if they would continue the sexual favors. When these patients' dependency conflicts were stirred up in the group, they felt compelled to terminate the treatment. Not surprisingly, they believed treatment was too expensive and used finances as a pretext for leaving the group precipitously.

Yet another role fluctuation these patients experience is between being "perverts" and "normal" individuals. They tend to idealize their picture of normal sexual life as rosy, romantic, and "virginal," as real sexuality is perceived as unhealthy. For example, one woman reacted intensely to the sound of the male therapist's breathing. She connected heavy breathing with sexual arousal, remembering sounds made by the adult who had sexually abused her. She implied that the therapist's breathing was perverse.

These adults oscillate also between appearing to be "sexual experts," with extensive sexual experience, and "shameful ignorants," who know nothing about sexual physiology and reality. As experts, they sometimes verbalize seductive messages. For example, when the male therapist complimented one patient on her appearance, she immediately said, "I'm free this evening." The same patient waited until the male therapist was absent from a session to ask a question about female sexual physiology, namely, whether being sexually aroused with a forbidden person is normal.

Sadomasochistic issues are important, as there is in incest an intertwining of love and abuse of power by the seducing adult. There are issues of domination versus submission, of being treated as a "piece of property" or a "possession" by the adult. The patients actually were victims of forceful seduction; as children, they could do nothing but respond with a mixture of passive compliance and, later, active exploitation. Passive compliance was the response of one patient, who as a child would pretend to be asleep when she heard her father's steps coming toward her bedroom. She would remain immobile while he performed his sexual acts. We heard from these patients many stories of exploitation involving force. One girl's father forced her at gunpoint to participate in sexual orgies with him and her siblings. Another patient's father forced her to go to school and recruit little girls to satisfy his pedophilic perversion. A third patient felt exploited by the therapists, who she thought made her attend the sessions in order to keep the group going. She could not agree with another member's conviction that she still had important psychotherapeutic work to accomplish. She claimed instead her alleged achievements in confronting her incestuous seducer.

Other members thought the therapists were really the ones who needed the group, not the patients! They relished pointing out and perpetuating the extremely tense, almost unbearable group atmosphere. They repeatedly stated how they wanted to spare themselves such discomfort by leaving the group. It was as if they were saying, "Mom wishes to cling to the illusion of us having a nice, united family, but the home atmosphere is rotten!"

These reciprocal roles lead to an identification with the aggressor. For instance, the same girl who as a child was forced at gunpoint into family sexual orgies, as an adult baits and lures men, dominating and exploiting them, not at gunpoint but by being very seductive. She acts as if she were ready to avenge herself on men by exploiting them as her father exploited her.

Incest victims' sexual relations with appropriate partners are disturbed because of their previous experience. These people may feel ashamed and perplexed at the differences of having sexual contact with an appropriate partner. They wonder whether to tell the truth about being victims of incest. They fear the absolute impossibility of ever reaching "normal" sexual relationships, which they imagine as romantic and almost sexless. Last, but not least, they suffer unbearable flashbacks of their perverse experiences. As in severe traumatic neurosis, the scenes of the traumas are replayed.

In society, the person with a childhood history of incest fluctuates between being "special" at home (or in court!) and an "outcast" with peers: the shift from being special to being one among many peers is like a demotion, a loss of status. Incestuous persons feel isolated from peers because of shame, guilt, and knowledge. Hence the peer group is lost as a resource for emotional growth. This role fluctuation is illustrated by a male patient we interviewed. He chose not to participate in the group and openly spoke with dread about anticipating the loss of being special. He was apprehensive about friends knowing his incestuous secret. He said he was indeed his mother's favorite and that she had given him the privilege of being a special individual. He anticipated he would resent any criticism of her by other group members.

The loss of the peer group is important from the viewpoint of group psychotherapy. The rationale for prescribing group therapy as the treatment of choice for incest survivors is that it provides a surrogate peer group in which members can deal with emotional difficulties derived from the incest and can catch up on their emotional growth.

In social situations these persons fluctuate between judging themselves "chronic liars" and having fantasies of being "honest informers" who one day will "tell the truth." Being a "chronic liar" is like being a psychopath, like living a charade; being an "honest informer" is to betray the loved one. "Telling the truth" also risks being responded to with disbelief or, worse, with the conviction that this behavior should be reported and legal action taken. These multilayered conflicts culminate in a confused loss of the self.

Unfortunately, incest survivors are often disappointed with justice, perhaps only barely keeping alive the faint hope that something can be done to correct their traumatic lives. One patient, having been impregnated by her father and forced to have an abortion, realized that her father was starting to "fool around" with her younger sister. She then decided to take legal action. The mockery of justice was that her father was placed on parole for a short time. However, this patient continues to advocate public education about incest so that injustices can be rectified.

Frequently these patients' parents, who have "dirty secrets" at home, are seen by the community as model citizens. This hypocrisy, plus the limitations and clumsiness of the legal system, leaves these patients feeling that they really cannot trust anyone—that hypocrisy is pervasive.

These roles are reenacted in the group. Patients sometimes identify themselves with their aggressors. They also elicit in therapists roles complementary to the ones they have assumed, effecting a role suction through projective identification. Therapists can be pushed into assuming these roles. For instance, voyeuristic curiosity can be stimulated by patients' stories, and conflicted responses can fluctuate between lust and repulsion. The male patient's seductive behavior with the female therapist made her wonder, "How good would he be in bed?"—while the male

therapist harshly condemned this mother surrogate for her un-
believable lust! Of course, these reactions are true across gender.
Whenever the male therapist responds to seductive messages conveyed by female patients, the anger at the offender is reenacted
in the female therapist's feelings.

Cotherapists' Countertransference Responses

We have been treating these victims of incest with concurrent
group and individual therapy because they often have brittle,
immature egos and are prone to act out their hostile and self-
destructive tendencies. Our concern is to protect them from such
actions by providing them new contexts in which to understand
themselves and an opportunity to verbalize feelings rather than
act on them. Because concurrent group and individual psychotherapy may complicate matters by allowing an ''institutional-
ized'' external splitting of the transference, we meet periodically
with the treaters in order to reduce such splitting and make therapeutic use of it. Sometimes we are able to achieve coordinated
interventions.

When we started planning for the group, we struggled with
what to call these patients. Victims? Survivors? Sexually abused?
Incestuous persons? While each describes an aspect of these patients, it misses others. For example, ''victim'' overlooks the
sadistic power these patients may exert over the people surrounding them. One patient in the group was certainly ''abused,'' but
she also had become a powerful person in her family. She managed the household accounts and reigned as the favorite. ''Survivor,'' by implication, compares the incest experience to being
in a concentration camp. Most incestuous persons fight valiantly
for psychological survival as their abusers forbid them autonomy,
but biological death is usually neither imminent nor threatened.
Equating the threat of psychological death with that of biological

death promotes an inaccurate view of the experience. There is also a judgmental message implicit in the language used in discussing abusers. Speaking of excusing, forgiving, or accusing them, or of accusing someone else, tends to omit the loving, parenting, and loyal aspects of the relationship between victim and offender.

Perhaps the most dominant emotional responses we experienced toward group members were those of revulsion and disbelief. In the history of the study of incest, disbelief is paramount. Many mental health professionals, hearing about incestuous experiences, tend to discredit the report. When one patient told us that her father sold her sexual favors to others—a farmer in a small community, he treated his daughter like a brood mare or cow—we could not believe her. We were shocked.

When the group was just starting, a sense of secrecy and confidentiality led us to extremes in trying to hide our patients' identities. We had fantasies that everyone in the building was peering into our waiting room. Early on we also had rescue fantasies similar to a manic reparation. We had sexual fantasies across gender, especially fantasies of possession, believing that these persons were really "sexually experienced." The male therapist thought, "Gee, this woman is like a refined courtesan," while the female therapist wondered whether a male patient would be a perfect lover. Both therapists experienced considerable countertransference guilt and anxiety about being lured by the seductiveness of these patients, who have been described by Herman and Schatzow (1983) as being "ripe for acting out with their therapists." Obviously, we were sad about their loneliness, realizing that these patients had had no effective parenting since they were six or seven years old and that they thought no one would ever believe them. Also, we were angry at the offenders, a reaction described by Boatman, Borkan, and Schetky (1981).

We experienced confusion over where to place love and loyalty, questioning whether incest is a matter simply of hate, abuse, and sadism. Gelinas (1983) admits a similar confusion. We also were surprised that the presenting complaint to clinicians is so frequently that of depression, anxiety, substance abuse, sexual difficulties, etc., and that clinicians usually have to learn of the incest by asking direct questions.

After six months of group meetings, a feeling of frustration set in. We realized that there was only hard work ahead, a very slow working through of a very complex problem. Our patients had to go through the complexity of a difficult struggle against pain, guilt, anger, and mistrust, but especially against denial. They needed to deny the loyalty, the love, and the enjoyment of their status as favorites; they needed to understand why incestuous acts sometimes had been fun; and they needed to work through their resentment at being rebuffed by the offender when he preferred a younger sister or some other woman. And then we had responded with our own mistrust (Poggi and Ganzarain, 1983), fearing we might be left to the mercy of these patients, who might sadistically avenge themselves on us, betraying us and doing to us what had been done to them. The cotherapist couple, after all, may easily become a transference surrogate for each patient's parents. The severely disturbed relations between these parents, and between them and their offspring, may be repeated in the group, providing opportunities for therapeutic work.

The risk of disruptive competition between the cotherapists is minimized by jointly dictating notes about each group meeting and discussing them together; by together planning strategies dealing with possible interventions, decisions, referrals, other helpers, publications, etc.; and by frequently discussing their feelings and differences, but without sharing these with the group.

During the sessions the therapists should not engage in verbal exchanges with each other, as this likely would interfere with or unnecessarily complicate the natural and spontaneous flow of the sessions. Instead they should explore their countertransference conflicts while discussing each session privately or with super-

visors. Sometimes these discussions begin as individual reflections which later on are shared with the other therapist.

As cotherapists we have often felt under attack, both from
patients and from other treaters who have tried to split us as a
couple. We agree with Corwin (1983) that this tendency to split
us, and to regard us as parents, may be used to therapeutic advantage. And of course we lend ourselves to this transference
casting. Like parents worried for their family, we experience
fears that the group will disintegrate, that members will drop out,
which is parallel to a child's abruptly leaving home in anger and
running away. And we tend to take refuge in our relationship
with each other against the many anxieties that occur when working with these difficult patients—our "children."

Cotherapists are of course cast in gender-related roles in the
transference. On the one hand, the female therapist may experience a feeling the mothers of her female patients may know:
"They're not telling me everything." She feels somewhat betrayed by the secret liaison going on between the female patients
and the male therapist. She is surprised by the absence of overt
anger toward her, though there is considerable nonverbal competition among the women involving clothes, hairdos, and per-
fume. She also senses that the patients devalue her and cast her
in the stereotypical role of "Mommy," who should inform them
about the facts of life. On the other hand, the male therapist feels
that he is the target of these patients' anger against men, whom
they see as potential abusers. Being angry, they indirectly rebuff
him with statements such as "I would fix that steer" when talking
about men who approach them. He feels also that he is the recipient of unconscious seductive messages, an experience observed by Fowler, Burns, and Roehl (1983).

(It might be noted here that when doctor-patient "incest"
occurs, it parallels the double betrayal of "natural" incest in that
an initial contract is broken and a helping relationship lost. The
second betrayal usually occurs later, when the love relationship

ends. There is initially the same secrecy, guilt, and excitement over being a favorite.)

Other Helpers' Responses to Incestuous Persons

Concurrent helpers (legal professionals or treaters such as individual psychotherapists, hospital staff, etc.) frequently respond to the influences group psychotherapists have over incestuous persons with competition and jealousy. There is competition among all the helpers, including the group psychotherapists, over who controls and possesses the case. Competition occurs also over who is the most effective, the most comprehensive, the most understanding, the most knowledgeable helper. Because they have been raised in homes where they were "special" in many ways, these patients evince the characteristics of the "special patient" syndrome so aptly described by Main (1957); thus, they may encourage splitting and promote competitiveness among their various treaters.

Jealousy can be the by-product of this competition. Incestuous persons often stimulate feelings of exclusion as they attempt to cope with their own sensitivity to being excluded. They may replicate in the therapeutic relationship a family situation in which issues of inclusion became paramount—the reversal of a situation across generations whereby children were excluded from the secrets of their parents' bedrooms.

Family therapists may have a special response to the incestuous person. To promote open communication within the family system, they may encourage the incestuous person to confront the offender before the entire family. Since such confrontation is a revenge fantasy frequently entertained by incestuous persons, they may accept this recommendation out of a wish for vengeance. It is debatable, then, whether incestuous persons should discuss the matter with the offender alone, share their secret with no one, or reveal it to the entire family. This subject was a matter of frequent discussion in our group. The consensus was that the decision belongs to each individual patient. However, a dramatic confrontation before the whole family frequently does not work, as the offender may deny any wrongdoing and family members may side with the offender, criticizing the victim or accusing him or her of being "crazy." Some family therapists recommend a step by step exploration of the incest situation: first the victim should talk with other siblings who have been victimized; then the matter should be discussed with the excluded parent; and finally the "hidden secret" should be talked about in a meeting with the entire family.

Discussion

Mental health professionals frequently respond with disbelief to patients who disclose incestuous experiences. The idea that Freud considered such confessions mere fantasies is often cited in support of such disbelief. In our view, however, Freud's position has been subject to a persistent misunderstanding; certainly he was one to acknowledge that childhood seduction (including incestuous seduction) in fact occurs. "Actual seduction . . . ," he wrote, "is common enough; it is initiated by . . . someone in charge of the child who wants to soothe it . . . or make it dependent on them. Where seduction intervenes it invariably disturbs the natural course of the developmental processes, and it often leaves behind extensive and lasting consequences" (Freud, 1931, p. 232). It is of course true that Freud's discovery of intrapsychic reality, the life of fantasy, as a determinant of mental symptoms so struck him, and so skewed the emphasis of his writings, as perhaps to obscure from inattentive readers the fact of actually occurring incest. (The spontaneous tendency in all of us to deny this unpleasant fact may well nourish this inattention.)

In reality, actual incest and incestuous fantasies are by no means mutually exclusive. The two may coexist, although incestuous fantasies occur in most instances in the absence of actual incest. But when actual incest is in fact the problem, therapists may feel confused by the many conflicting feelings the person experiences. This confusion may become unbearable for the therapist. In an effort to avoid chaos, clinicians may artificially narrow their focus, ignoring the complexity of the problem, and adopt stereotypes in an effort to understand it. For instance, we initially referred to our patients simply as "victims," thus ignoring the fact that they also had experiences whereby they felt themselves to be powerful, the rulers of their homes. By emphasizing the masochistic aspects of victimization, we had overlooked the sadistic power that persons subjected to incest may exert over the people surrounding them.

The description of the incestuous experience as a trauma uses the conceptual framework of traumatic neurosis. Indeed, these patients do experience "flashbacks" of traumatic scenes and suffer other symptoms typical of traumatic neurosis. But some incestuous experiences are not painful. In fact, most incest situations have their pleasurable aspects. Specifically, incestuous relationships may include love and loyalty. In addition, mutual gratification may be involved, though clinicians and patients alike have difficulty acknowledging that incest may occasion satisfaction.

Sometimes, because pain is not present, incestuous experiences fail to trigger intense anxiety and defensiveness. The child may think that such sexual activity happens in every family, may feel torn between curiosity and surprise, and may passively comply. When the trauma becomes chronic, however, certain dysphoric feelings predictably appear. The adult partner wishes to keep the child as is, without allowing growth. The child, however, gradually discovering that this situation is not "normal," struggles to become disentangled from a situation that has become habitual.

The complex network of interactions in the incestuous couple is repeated in the transference. The therapists' blindness to aspects of the transference may promote their being acted out. Acting out may also be stimulated by the therapists' countertransference reactions, which may blind them to the complete picture. If these reactions trap the therapist in a simplistic, categorizing view of the patient's experience, whatever is omitted will likely be acted out. For instance, an overemphasis on sexual behavior may lead to a neglect of the sadistic component, so that the patient uses sexual attractiveness to sadistically dominate the partner.

Concurrent group and individual psychotherapy (as well as psychiatric hospitalization, when indicated) may externalize the intrapsychic splitting. Different aspects of the patient's pathology may be revealed in the various treatment modalities. If it is possible to establish collaborative relationships among the various treaters, the destructive consequences of this externalized splitting may be counteracted. Patients may then have an opportunity to achieve a fully integrated view of the many conflicts involved in the problem of incest. Integrating the different aspects of the self will eventually occur within the patient's mind.

We wish to emphasize that it took considerable effort to sort out what these patients elicited in us. Our difficulties were somehow comparable to overcoming the effects of prejudice, but these feelings were stronger than even racism and sexism. These patients had broken a taboo, and we could not remain indifferent to their transgression. We kept wondering unconsciously whether they were victims, monsters, or heroes.

Revulsion and disbelief sometimes prevented us from asking questions and listening in an effective and helpful manner. Our guilt, fear, and discomfort combined to create resistances in communicating openly and empathically with these patients. In short, we frequently felt deskilled by our responses when treating the emotional scars of incest.

Chapter 2

Transference When Incest Is the Problem

In this chapter we describe the typical transferences of incest victims treated in long-term psychoanalytic group therapy. The literature on incest contains little in the way of systematic description of the transference characteristics of these patients.

As a basic psychotherapeutic concept, transference was discovered by Sigmund Freud (1905, 1912, 1914b). He defined it as the displacement of wishes and affects regarding a person in an individual's past to a current substitute who awakens the same conflicted wishes and feelings.

Advances in psychoanalytic theory have led to the discovery of new aspects of transference. For instance, with the development of the structural theory, the psychoanalyst was also viewed as a substitute, by projection, for the patient's prohibiting parental figures, already internalized in the patient's superego. The study of object relations promoted the view that the analytic situation is a repetition of the early mother-child relationship. Research on ego psychology increased the importance attributed to the defensive processes an individual uses to avoid anxiety. Thus

17

may the various aspects of transference be better understood using the appropriate psychoanalytic theories.

Other new aspects of transference were revealed as psychoanalytic therapy was applied to different types of patient. The analytic treatment of children and psychotic patients showed the importance of the ambivalent preoedipal relationship with the mother, a relationship repeated in the therapeutic situation. Similarly, the psychotherapeutic treatment of patients with narcissistic personality disorder led to the description of a special "narcissistic" transference (Kohut, 1968) wherein the therapist is treated as a "self-object."

Whether transference requires well-integrated, mature ego functions, and whether psychoanalytic psychotherapy can occur in the absence of a mature ego, are related questions that have occasioned violent polemics. As intense regressions occur in group psychotherapy, we should ask ourselves whether regression is a resistance (Zetzel, 1956) or a deepening of treatment that allows the exploration of early anxieties?

When applied to psychoanalytic group therapy, the concept of transference requires further examination, most notably because the transference targets are multiple: therapists (one or two), other members, and the group as an entity. The presence of various targets raises the question of transference "dilution" as well as the issue of whether a complete "transference neurosis" can develop in the group setting.

Bion (1961) described the emotional life of the individual in a group as comparable to the infant's experience of early psychotic-like anxieties when first dealing with the breast. He thus postulated a part-object transference from the breast to an abstract entity, the group-as-a-whole. He also described how primitive defense mechanisms, such as projective identification and splitting, prevail as defensive operations in groups. Regarding projective identification, Bion's disciple Ezriel (1950) stated that "When several people meet in a group, each member projects his own unconscious fantasy-objects upon various other group members and then tries to manipulate them accordingly" (p. 62). Regarding transference in psychoanalysis and in groups, he wrote somewhat later (Ezriel, 1952) that while patient and analyst started historically, working like "two friendly archaeologists trying to dig up the patient's past, they became later on two human beings interacting with one another in the here-and-now, according to the latter's unconscious fantasies" (p. 120).

Thus, according to Ezriel, each patient is also the recipient of multiple projective identifications from other group members, so that each is pushed into assuming certain roles, or is coerced by group "role suction" (Redl, 1963) into adopting characteristic patterns. Specific behaviors automatically invite complementary responses or roles. For instance, a member's exhibitionistic behaviors are an invitation for the others to look, or masochistic needs become an invitation for others to injure, dominate, or abuse.

In chapter 1, on countertransference, we have described some typical group roles assumed by persons with a history of incest. These patients learn specific roles in their families, and they repeat such behaviors in the transference. They suffered a deficit of adequate parenting and were forced to act as parents to their own parents. They are confused about their identity, not knowing whether to act like sexual grown-ups or like children in need of nurturance. They show a mixture of sadism and loving care, alternately attempting to seduce or dominate others, or fearfully submitting to them. They fluctuate between feeling "special" (at home) or like outcasts (with peers), haunted by shame and guilt because of their dark secret.

Varieties of Transference

In psychotherapy for incest the initial focus is on the trauma, thereby casting the abuser in the role of villain. In the cases we treated, the perpetrator was usually a male. The target of the patient's early anger was therefore the father or brother, while the mother stayed in the shadows, out of focus. The first explorations of the trauma lead naturally to a catharsis of anger during which the therapist supports the patient by reinforcing defenses. In short-term therapies, this ventilation of rage may be the major goal. Because these women's relationships with men are permeated with anger, the transference is usually negative when the therapist is male. By contrast, when the therapist is female, the transference is positive and rage is then concentrated in relationships with important male figures in the patient's life. The ventilation of rage is thus extratransferential.

However, when more ambitious goals are pursued within a long-term treatment, rage at the mother eventually becomes prominent. Only as the daughter's conflicted relationship with her mother is explored do the deep mistrust, deprivation, and guilt that permeate the interpersonal relationships of all these patients become evident. These severe maternal conflicts may undermine therapy, just as they have limited the patient's past relationships.

Most patients find it much easier to focus on how angry they are at their male abusers than to acknowledge the full extent of their disappointment and sense of betrayal regarding their mothers. They therefore feel compelled either to end treatment prematurely (once the rage at males has been ventilated) or to remain fixated in fury toward men to avoid awareness of more painful feelings. The rage at males may be secondarily magnified as an unconscious defensive maneuver.

In what follows we will explore three varieties of transference: parental (paternal and maternal), sibling, and group-as-a-whole.

Parental Transferences

Differentiating maternal from paternal transferences is often difficult because of the confusion of roles in the family of origin.

There are frequently indistinct differentiations between mother and father, child and parents, male and female. In many cases of father-daughter incest, the mother was absent or nonfunctional; hence the father assumed a variety of maternal roles while the abused daughter, usually the oldest, was pushed into becoming a mother surrogate for her younger siblings.

These confusions of family roles are compounded by the unconscious human proclivity to develop fantasies that confuse genders. Such fantasies include images of the phallic mother ("the witch") or displacement of oral needs from the mother's breast to the father's penis. Thus, oral needs may be disguised in what appears to be genitally organized behavior; e.g., a small girl needs to be loved and may appear coquettish in an attempt to obtain that love.

Paternal transference. In our group psychotherapy for women with a history of incest, paternal transference is clear because there is only one man present—the male therapist. On one occasion Karen responded to the absence of the female therapist by remembering the direct sexual invitation her father extended to her and her two sisters. While driving back home with them, having left their mother at the airport, he asked, "Which one of you girls will sleep with Dad tonight?" In this session, interestingly, the only people present were the male therapist and three patients (all of course female).

Frequently the paternal transference has a sadomasochistic flavor. Mary, for example, left therapy prematurely in a replay of her relationship with her father. He had attempted to subjugate her by giving her money for living expenses at college in exchange for sexual intercourse, but she rebuffed his attempts by leaving home at a very young age. During her treatment, she interpreted fee negotiations as an attempt by the therapists to subjugate her as her father had, so she left the therapy.

Jane provided another instance of how the paternal transference may have overtones of sadomasochism. When Jane entered the group, she presented herself as having repaired her relationship with her abusive father to the point that they now enjoyed one another appropriately. As the other group members gradually indicated their disbelief that the relationship was so "healthy," Jane redoubled her efforts to portray how satisfactory it really was. However, by presenting herself as having progressed further than the others, she set herself up to be attacked, replicating a characteristic style of interaction whereby she provoked her father's criticism and then submitted to him. In a later session Jane became aware of her tendency to relate in this style. When another member demanded an apology from the male therapist, Jane acknowledged her hope that an apology would be forthcoming, despite her disagreement with the demand. She then realized that an apology from the male therapist was important to her because she wished him to submit to the other patient, just as she wished that she could subjugate her father.

There are observable divisions within the paternal transference. One split is sexual versus nurturing, contingent upon whether the father is seen as a genital stimulus or as a caring figure, while another is a division along sadistic and masochistic lines. Such splits may challenge rigid paternal transference stereotypes.

Maternal transference. Expecting and obtaining support and understanding is at first the natural maternal transference paradigm: "For emergencies, call Momma." At the beginning of therapy the negative maternal transference is therefore elusive and the intricate nuances of ambivalence can easily be overlooked. In the background, however, the preoedipal features of the relationship with mother silently prevail. Characteristically present, for instance, are anger over maternal deprivation, envy of the mother's power, and a fear of becoming overdependent. This last issue may often be disguised by a pretense of self-sufficiency that counters the pain of having lost the mother as a source of nurture.

Maternal transference is elusive also because of confusion over whether oedipal or preoedipal transferences prevail. In our group of female patients oedipal rivalry with mother figures may be only superficial; often the preoedipal components are the more important and problematic parts of the maternal transference. A wish that the mother were omnipotent and all-powerful alternates with envy of her perceived power, and the reception of psychological nurturance is thereby obstructed. Preoedipal and genital aspects, dependency on and devaluation of maternal images, and counterdependent envious struggles against the need to be nurtured are all intertwined.

Perceptions of the mother as "safe" or "worthy of competition" are countered by verbal characterizations of her as "weak" or otherwise flawed. One member of the group, Wilma, complained that the female therapist always made comments that were "off base." Betty shared her perception of the female therapist as weak, fragile, and easily hurt. As Betty continued to study for her college degree, she became openly critical of both therapists' group techniques, labeling them "old-fashioned, rigid, and ineffectual."

The initial conflict over the need to be cared for by the mother is frequently evidenced in interactions with the group, as will be seen in the case of Anna. This will be followed by a vignette involving Betty which illustrates the reenactment, within a sexual relationship, of dependency conflicts with a mother.

Anna is convinced her mother does not care for her. Whenever Anna attempts to share important matters with her, her mother changes the subject. However, Anna professes to not need her mother's care, since her husband is "very maternal." Yet she repeatedly seeks contact with her mother.

In one group session Anna began by reporting an encounter with her mother. Group members attempted to help her by observing that Anna's angry, confrontational approach might make her mother feel guilty. But Anna was unable to acknowledge her anger. The group went on to suggest again that Anna's mother may feel guilty. Anna responded that she knew it. She then forthrightly denied her yearnings for her mother's affection. The group confronted her about her repeated efforts to receive nurturance from her mother, despite her awareness that it would not be forthcoming. Anna's rejections of group attempts to help her duplicated the disappointment that pervaded interactions with her mother. The group felt it had failed, and Anna had a sense of paradoxical triumph in having proven, once again, how inadequate nurturing figures really are.

Then Betty related her most recent disappointment with her lover. Sex with him was unsatisfying because of premature ejaculation. When she complained to him, he suggested having sex daily to overcome the problem. Betty was infuriated by this loss of control over their sexual life. Though she did not wish to have daily sex in order to have her needs satisfied, she agreed resentfully and their sexual life improved. However, still angry because she felt controlled by her boyfriend, she occasionally made herself a passive sexual partner, feeling irritated and contemptuous. Another member laughingly suggested that Betty should tell him "to satisfy himself in the bathroom." In Betty's mind a role reversal had occurred whereby the lover was now the needy one, under her control, while she triumphantly despised him. The group atmosphere was manic.

There were significant parallels between Anna's relationship with her mother and Betty's interaction with her boyfriend. The therapists commented that Betty was treating her lover the way Anna treats her mother: both denied their dependency needs and their guilt about being overdemanding, and both reversed roles, making the other person the needy one. Group members laughed, mocking those more needy than they. Such joyful excitement —while it lasted—made further therapeutic work impossible. The therapists' intervention was followed by a brief period of reflection, and then by an intensification of the manic mood. The typical manic style of treating others with contempt, control, and triumph was extended from Anna's mother and Betty's lover to the therapists. The solutions they offered were devalued as insufficient and poorly timed; the patients exerted their control by deciding not to accept these solutions. In this they felt they had defeated the other person's attempt to help them. Envy of the powerful and gratifying breast or penis part-object thus leads to its triumphant devaluation by rejecting the satisfaction it offers.

Another way in which the initial conflict over the need to be cared for by the mother is repeated in the relationship with the group is seen in the case of Wilma. Wilma's mother is mentally dysfunctional, intermittently psychotic; she often confuses Wilma with her other daughter. As at times she is unable to care for herself, Wilma must mother her own mother. This leaves Wilma feeling frustrated, longing for maternal care. These unfulfilled yearnings are so strong that from time to time she discounts her mother's limitations and tries once again to give her mother another chance: she phones her or invites her for a weekend visit. Sometimes she even tries to talk with her mother about the family experience of incest. Needless to say, most of the time she ends up frustrated once again.

Wilma is attached to the group but repeatedly expresses dissatisfaction with it. She feels misunderstood by the therapists and claims to be indifferent to the absence of either. She ignores the ideas put forth by the female therapist but responds significantly to the affective aspects of her comments, as if to say, "Mom, I know your brain is lost but I yearn for your heart." Similarly, she reports in the group sessions that she frequently feels misunderstood or ignored by her individual therapist. On one occasion she added that after seeing him she sometimes gets drunk. She reflected that just before phoning him late at night she had the thought that what she really wanted was her mother.

Like other patients in the group, Wilma repeats the conflict with her mother in her relationship with her sexual partner. She mothers him as she would like to be mothered herself—a "narcissistic object choice" (Freud, 1914a)—and as she mothers her own mother. As a child, she learned to take care of her parents and to become her own mother. Her maternal deprivation, however, is ongoing, as is her devaluation of her mother.

These patients devalue the mother in a variety of ways. She is seen as sexually inadequate, ethically unreliable, and financially disorganized. Sometimes these perceptions are at least partially based on fact. One of our patients knows, for instance, that her mother became sexually inactive following an accident in which her pelvis was crushed. Another is aware that her mother stopped sexual activity to avoid further pregnancies when the patient was eight years old. A transferential aspect of this devaluation is seen in the failure of our group patients to acknowledge the sexuality of the female therapist; for example, the fact that she is married is never addressed, although one group member has had significant professional contact with the therapist's husband.

In the view of these patients, their mothers abdicated their ethical responsibility by allowing them to be used sexually by other family members. Some wonder if their mothers had unconsciously or even consciously colluded in the intrafamily sexual abuse. Each believes that her mother preferred the abuser to the victimized child, a preference which might have led to the mother's covertly lenient attitude toward the abuser's sexual activities. In addition to feeling unprotected by their mothers, the victimized children felt that their mothers were not emotionally available. As a result, feelings of jealousy, exclusion, and loneliness accumulated.

Unclear family rules and a lack of precise boundaries led to the formation in these patients of consciences, or superegos, that are weak, confusing, unpredictable, and sometimes overly punitive. On one occasion when the female therapist was absent, the patients felt abandoned and reacted dramatically. They felt as if the female therapist had left them unprotected, and they felt vulnerable to potential abuse at the hands of the male therapist. Being left alone with father is still unbearably threatening.

Several members of the group viewed their mothers as financially troubled. One member had literally run the family finances while her mother was psychotic. Others saw their mothers as the breadwinners—struggling, overworking, yet never providing enough money. Within the group it has been difficult to discuss financial matters, especially fees. Each session, two members bring payments to the group and, without explanation, consistently hand their checks to the female therapist. It is as if they perceive her as the one who needs the money and who should be in charge of finances. By contrast, the members deal with the male therapist regarding fees mainly when they need to renegotiate a lower fee (e.g., Betty tried to have a private meeting with him with this agenda in mind).

The therapist couple. In our group there has been little discussion about how the members view the therapists as a couple. Particularly noticeable is the absence of verbalized sexual fantasies about them. Hence the discussion that follows is for the most part speculative.

As we have mentioned, two of our patients have information about their parents as sexually dysfunctional couples. The parents of several other members were divorced, a fact easily leading to fantasies that their parents' sexual relationships were disturbed. Thus the stage is set for these patients to transfer to the cotherapist couple the image of a sexually dysfunctional parental couple.

Oedipal fantasies and conflicts could be surmised—and were sometimes observed—when inhibiting or stimulating sexual impulses toward the cotherapists appeared and the patients competed unconsciously to gain the favor of one of them, or to split the couple and become the focus of heterosexual or homosexual preference. An example of homosexually tinged transference occurred when the male therapist was a few minutes late for a session. Betty anxiously assumed that the female therapist would become so worried about the male therapist that she would be unable to pay attention to the group, to herself in particular. Betty then remembered her father's frequent absences or late arrivals at the dinner table, which caused her mother to be upset and emotionally unavailable to the children. As Betty kept on talking in an effort to occupy the female therapist's attention, the rivalry between her and her father for the mother's affection was clearly reenacted.

The cotherapist couple may also be perceived as a father-daughter couple, either an ideally normal one or a secretly incestuous one. When perceived as a normal father-daughter couple, they may be admired or envied, their interactions observed but not openly discussed. Patients who view them as an incestuous couple may feel that secrecy is necessary, and their efforts to maintain it both protect and devalue the cotherapist couple.

Sibling Transference

Each member of the group perceives the others as adolescent peers or siblings. Growing up with a dark secret, isolated from friends at school and in the neighborhood, has left a void. These patients lack the experience of having peers as "best friends." The psychotherapy group provides delayed compensation for this lack but also fosters a proclivity to idealize the group as "best friends."

By contrast, ambivalence characterizes the sibling transference. When the father was the abuser and two or more sisters were victimized, guilt and competition prevail. Guilt is induced by not having met a sister's expectations for protection, rescue, or cooperation in stopping the abuse.

In the group, peer cohesiveness increased when members perceived the therapists as the common enemy. Members spent time together outside the group meetings, attended shows as a group, and explored the possibility of firing the therapists or moving as a group to another agency. Likewise, when the issue of confronting one's sexual abuser was raised, these patients actively exchanged experiences and supported one another; together they examined the pros and cons and the difficulties in such confrontations. One member was given supervision as she confronted her abuser about his past behavior. The atmosphere was similar to that of a group of adolescent girls advising one another about dating relationships.

Sibling transference when the father was the offender brings up a serious challenge to these patients' perceptions of themselves as unique or "special." In the group, they have to learn to live with others who are also "unique" individuals, who also had unusual, forbidden sexual experiences. Here competitive struggles for attention may take the form of vying for recognition as the most brutally victimized or the most emotionally disturbed. One member who was abused by her father cherished the impression that she was special to the male therapist. She believed he had created the group out of a wish to help her. Wilma became intensely jealous of Jane when she learned they shared the same gynecologist. Jane's obvious wealth increased Wilma's jealousy. Shortly thereafter she observed that Jane reminded her of her own younger sister, who had replaced her as her father's "mistress."

Several members of the group came from families where the father abused more than one daughter. One was an older sister's replacement. Three were themselves replaced by younger sisters. These three experienced a tremendous conflict between relief that the father had focused his sexual interest on another daughter and guilt over having sacrificed the younger sister. Karen's sister died mysteriously shortly after Karen left home. Karen wonders if she killed herself because of sexual victimization when Karen was absent and unable to rescue her. Wilma's sister now lives a chaotic life. But because Wilma attempted to rescue her sister by reporting their father to the police, she feels she has expiated her guilt for abandoning her sister. Thus she is relatively less uncomfortable discussing this matter in the group. Karen, by contrast, avoids exploring the issue, but reacts nonverbally to circumstances that remind her of her guilt (e.g., she was cool and aloof in response to the friendly overtures of Jane, when Jane was acting self-destructively).

Jealousy fuels the guilt over having damaged a sister, insofar as rivalry with that sister may induce the wish to eliminate her as a competitor. In the group, jealousy and rivalry come to the fore when a new group member arrives. For instance, Martha came late for her first meeting with the group. While most of the members assumed that we wanted the meeting to begin with the arrival of the new person, Betty announced that she would use the time before Martha's arrival to discuss a problem: how much she needs to be in control. (The members had openly opposed the addition of a new member, so obviously the decision to add Martha was not under their control.) When Martha arrived, the group was reacting intensely to our observation that they all had a need to be in control. As she sat down, there was a long silence. One of us remarked that maybe the silence was the expression of mixed feelings about the addition of a new member. Competition ensued over who would dominate the meeting, either by attempting to organize the remainder of the time, or by reporting the most dramatic example of victimization; attempts to recruit Martha as an ally were also evident. For the first time, Betty hinted guiltily that she might have contributed to her younger sister's sexual abuse, joining her brothers in seducing the sister to participate in their sexual group activities. Betty's concern could be translated into the here and now as a glimmering awareness of current wishes to hurt the "youngest" group member.

Since the group has no male members, we have been unable to explore direct sister-brother transference. However, the male therapist has on occasion been cast in the role of an offending brother. There are also occasional hints of homosexually tinged intermember transferences in which the male therapist appears as a rival for the female therapist's attention.

Group-as-a-Whole Transference

The group as an entity has mothering functions providing a maternal holding environment, so that omissions and errors in the childhood relationship with the mother may be partially compensated. The group-mother believes and understands the awful secret of incest and its appalling consequences. This surrogate mother loves the patients and lets them know they are worthy of being loved. The group provides company, encouragement, and support for members who are seriously ill. For example, when Karen had a gallbladder attack, members supported her with calls and visits. The group becomes a surrogate mother who is always available, a mother on whom members can rely when in need. For instance, when Karen moved from one residence to another, she requested and received assistance from other members. And one Thanksgiving evening, when Wilma felt alone and depressed, realizing she had missed in life the usual family experiences associated with holidays, she longed for her mother and wished to call her. She decided, however, not to phone her mother and instead called another group member.

The group can also specifically compensate for defects in the superego development of its members. All of them grew up in a family atmosphere fraught with lying, mistrust, betrayal, and deceptions; they grew up without a consistent sense of right and wrong. In these families parents did not perform the ordinary function of teaching ethical norms. Because these parents were perceived as corrupt, the rules they established were questionable and subject to challenge. Thus, while the cotherapists—cast in these parental roles—seem to lack moral reliability, the group-as-a-whole is by contrast trustworthy and will be listened to. That was the case when Ingrid shared with the group her struggles over whether she should confront her abuser and terminate their relationship. She believed that he deserved punishment for abusing her, and that the entire family, immediate and extended, should learn of his cruelty. Group members acknowledged the offender's obvious guilt, but repeatedly helped Ingrid realize that revenge motivated her to construct cruel confrontation scenarios. Because her sadistic superego cruelly blamed her, she wished to punish the offender similarly. She was prone to confuse negotiations aimed at terminating the incestuous relationship with a "trial" to punish the offender. Such confusion might have led to painful self-defeat had the group not helped her plan a private and successful meeting.

On another occasion, the group helped Wilma recognize and terminate a self-destructive behavior. Wilma had betrayed her spouse by taking a lover. She felt she needed additional love and care, and seemed unaware of the self-destructive implications of the situation. She could lose her husband and was allowing herself to be abused by her demanding and neurotic lover. Patiently and firmly, the group told Wilma that she was risking her marriage and humiliating herself. This advice was not judgmental but loving and understanding, like that given by a good maternal superego. Wilma was then able to end her relationship with her lover in a thoughtful, mature way.

But the group-as-a-whole can also be perceived as a replica of the dysfunctional family of origin: unreliable, uncaring, and chaotic. The parents could not be relied on to protect and guide the children by setting appropriate limits. Because parental needs took precedence when the incest occurred, the children were left with a feeling that their parents did not care for them. The incest was just another expression of their parents' self-centeredness, which prevented the parents from being attuned to their children's needs. Role confusion creates a chaotic emotional atmosphere in these families: parents behave as if they are still children and elicit parentlike behavior from their offspring. In addition to not assuming normal family roles, parents shift roles from one extreme to another. They may abruptly stop behaving like children who need to be taken care of, and reassume rigid parenting roles. The unpredictability of these sudden shifts adds to the confusion. Families with special characteristics, such as single-parent families or those in extreme poverty (with mothers working several jobs), can exacerbate the family disorganization. In the course of its development every psychotherapy group has periods when it may seem unreliable, uncaring, and chaotic. Whenever these periods occurred in our group, members reexperienced situations originally encountered in their families of origin. As noted in chapter 1, this made some of our patients feel an urgent need to leave the group precipitously, much as they may have left their families.

Discussion

The basic transference of these patients is maternal and preoedipal, repeating early relations with part-objects; this fact may mislead clinicians into assuming that the patients belong to just one psychiatric diagnostic category (i.e., borderline personality organization). However, as a result of primitive struggles common to early development, preoedipal conflicts and part-object transferences are present in every human being. Thus, borderline-like phenomena appear in every psychotherapy that reaches any depth. Some patients do in fact meet the criteria for a diagnosis of borderline personality disorder, but other diagnoses, such as multiple personality, anorexia nervosa, depression, may also be made. What makes psychopathology so dramatic in this patient population is a combination of severe family pathology and intense trauma, sometimes lasting for years.

Confusion of roles within the families of these patients was pervasive. They were perplexed about how to meet their family's expectations. Likewise, their view of themselves fluctuated among many contradictory roles. In their families of origin, gender-related roles were frequently confused. Often the father was the nurturant, maternal parent. In contemporary families, many couples share equally in child-caring functions, but the father does not share these tasks because the mother is dysfunctional; she is available when needed. In incestuous families, however, the mother was often unavailable and sometimes dysfunctional, leaving a void of maternal deprivation for all family members. This deficit in maternal care is repeated in the transference.

The composition of our group differs from the usual in that there are no male members. Groups are ordinarily composed of men and women, and the presence of both sexes keeps the subject of sexual interaction at the center of the group's attention. Frequently intermember transactions have important sexual overtones. Moreover, members often project their own sexual urges onto the cotherapist couple, unconsciously attempting to induce them to act out the patients' libidinal fantasies. The psychodynamic tensions generated by the sexually mixed group are almost absent in this group of female members where the only man is a cotherapist. Discussions of sexual topics are colored by a regressive tendency to relate to men in a sadomasochistic or passive-dependent style. There was little mention within the group of primal scene fantasies involving the actual parental couple or the therapists viewed as a couple. The occasional transferential references to such fantasies had a sadomasochistic flavor accompanied by fears of violent disruptions within the therapist couple, as if in the patients' minds such ruptures heralded a recurrence of the sexual abuse they had suffered earlier. The resultant anxiety led them to avoid steadfastly any direct discussion of what they fantasied as the therapist couple's difficult relationship. Since these patients have gratified their oedipal yearnings instead of renouncing them, they are left with a legacy of guilt and a justifiable conviction that their parents do not get along well but need to ignore their difficulties. To cope with their pain, the parents combined avoidance with a variety of impulsive actions, including the sexual abuse of their children. Such unconscious convictions permeate the transferences of these patients.

In closing, we cite the words of Jung (1946) on the relation between incest and transference:

> The existence of the incest element involves . . . an emotional complication of the therapeutic situation. It is the hiding place for all the most secret, painful, intense, delicate, shame-faced, timorous, grotesque, immoral, and at the same time the most sacred feelings that make up the indescribable and inexplicable wealth of human relationships and give them their compelling power. Like the tentacles of the octopus, they twine themselves . . . through the transference, around doctor and patient. This binding force shows itself . . . in the patient's desperate clinging to the world of infancy or to the doctor. The word possession describes the state in a way that could hardly be better. [p. 179]

Chapter 3

Acting Out During Group Psychotherapy for Incest Victims

"Acting out" refers to behaviors during the course of psychotherapy that are characterized by the patient's acting instead of thinking, talking, or reflecting about feelings and attitudes. These actions take place primarily outside the therapy. But they may also occur within the therapeutic context. The proneness to act instead of reflect is then called "acting in."

Both "acting out" and "acting in" occur outside the patient's awareness of their meaning. Impulsive ways of avoiding full awareness of an emotional problem, these behaviors are at the same time attempts at communicating messages about painful conflicts.

Psychoanalysis values insight over abreaction but acknowledged early in its history that transference is essentially a repetition of early conflicts, rather than a remembering of them. It discovered that the interpretation of transference is a potent therapeutic tool that allows patients to recover their forgotten pasts and offers the opportunity to choose new and more adaptive ways of behaving, thereby resolving old conflicts. From this perspective, acting out may be seen as the consequence of incomplete

37

analysis of the transference (A. Freud, 1968); the patient's actions remain outside the therapeutic context because the impulses discharged have not been brought to conscious awareness.

Patients use projection and splitting, respectively, to "externalize" or to "divide and conquer" transference-related mental responses (fantasies, feelings) anxiously experienced as unacceptable. Likewise, when mental pain such as shame, anxiety, guilt, or sadness threatens these patients' well-being, they may deny such pain by frantically resorting to impulsive actions. Some activities will make them feel "happily excited" (e.g., "partying," enjoying sex and drugs) instead of sad; others may bring them to angrily blame and fight "enemies" or abusers to protect themselves from self-reproach or loneliness. In other words, hypomanic defenses such as omnipotent denial, or taking a paranoid stance, protect them from depression experienced as sadness and guilt.

Victims frequently identify themselves with their abusers, behaving like them vis-à-vis other helpless victims or adopting their abuser's attitudes and values. This paradoxical development is an instance of the defense mechanism of "identification with the aggressor."

Acting out has a bad connotation. There is a prejudice against it, as if it were no more than the product of faulty psychotherapeutic technique, or as if it must always have irreversible and damaging consequences. The truth is that acting out is in addition an incipient attempt to communicate unbearably painful mental contents that cannot reach consciousness (Grinberg, 1968) and can be discharged only as spontaneous actions (O'Shaughnessy, 1983). Acting out is like a dream that cannot be dreamt (Grinberg, 1968). Viewed in this perspective, acting out is a coded message from the patient's unconscious. Its content is elaborately disguised to pass through—to be "smuggled" across—the censorship that denies these contents access to consciousness. Psychotherapists are trained to decode such secret messages from the unconscious, but sometimes the code remains secret for quite a while. Patients may hurt themselves in the meantime, before the code is deciphered. Such is the unavoidable drama of acting out. One may find consolation, however, in knowing that actions will be repeated, in renewed attempts to get the cryptic messages across, until patient and psychotherapist alike are ready to deal with them.

Both patients and therapists need to reach a certain readiness to deal with the unconscious meaning of acting out. The facile advice sometimes given at psychiatric hospitals to acting out patients—to "talk instead of acting"—overlooks the very real difficulties patients have in choosing between actions and words to express their mental suffering. Verbalizing requires a sufficient working through of the depressive position. The depressive position is itself a major developmental achievement which makes possible symbolization and the labeling of feelings (Segal, 1974). Only after this mental growth has been achieved can mental contents be "put into words" (O'Shaughnessy, 1983). If the patient has not yet reached the depressive position, therapists who break "the secret code of acting out" will find the patient unprepared to understand fully the messages from the unconscious that they have translated.

Patients need to translate the therapist's words into their own language. To put the message into their own words requires a new integration of their mental contents, a product of working through the depressive position. Insight without new mental integration is only "pseudo" or incomplete insight, a limited, merely intellectual understanding by the patient of unconscious material. Frequently this pseudoinsight is a mere "parroting" of the psychotherapist's words, with no translation into the patient's own language.

Working through deserves attention as the most effective solution to the problem of acting out. Working through is a sort of psychical work that allows the patient to accept certain repressed elements and be freed from the grip of repetition (La-planche and Pontalis, 1973). It is necessary to supplement the focus on intrapsychic obstacles with a consideration of the therapist's contributions to this process. As Melanie Klein (1961) wrote, the task of the analyst is to "draw conclusions from the analytic material as it reappears in different contexts, and is accordingly interpreted" (p. 12). Psychotherapy groupmates may also contribute to each other's working through (Ganzarain, 1983).

Acting Out in Group Psychotherapy

Publications on the subject of acting out in group psychotherapy are scarce. The current literature tends to take a "cookbook" approach, focusing on one or more techniques believed to be effective in coping with this phenomenon. There is a general consensus that acting out should be interpreted in groups, as in any psychotherapy (Levy, 1984). There is some disagreement, however, regarding the setting of limits to inappropriate behavior. Levy maintains that interpretation by itself should suffice. Others (Ormont, 1969; Borriello, 1973, 1979) say that directly limiting acting out behavior is sometimes necessary. All agree, however, that acting out requires immediate attention. Borriello believes that this should include putting the affective experience into words. Soliciting the assistance of group members in understanding and interpreting the acting out is recommended.

The special aspects of acting out in psychotherapy groups are seldom explored in the literature. For instance, the availability of the patient's peers in acting out is seldom discussed, although it seems logical that this facet of group treatment would have a direct effect on acting out behavior (Rutan and Stone, 1984).

There are a number of reasons for the difficulty group psychotherapists have in discussing this subject. A popular notion about group psychotherapy is that it is an arena for wild sexual or aggressive behavior. Marmor (1972) refers to this belief when he states that some people come to group treatment consciously seeking erotic experiences. Hoping to disconfirm this mythology, group therapists may avoid altogether any discussion of acting out. Other authors label some forms of acting out as "practicing" (Yalom, 1975), thereby not only dispelling the myth but giving the behavior an adaptive connotation. Discussion of the issue may also be limited because therapists mistake a "flight into health" for true working through.

When we began our psychotherapy group with victims of incest, we asked ourselves: "will acting out become a problem in this group? Does incest produce a proclivity for acting out?" Since victims of incest frequently suffer from traumatic neuroses, and since mastery of trauma is achieved through repetition, a proclivity for acting out is to be expected. Bloch and Bloch (1976) have noted that acting out occurs in many patients suffering post-traumatic stress disorder.

The incest trauma leads to feelings of depression which are in turn defended against by denial and avoidance. Jumping into action is an easily invoked type of avoidance. In short, rather than becoming depressed and blaming themselves, these patients have a tendency either to become hypomanic deniers or to get paranoid and fight their abusers.

We shall discuss three areas of acting out in the course of group therapy for victims of incest: sex; power and sadism; and self-destructiveness. These three areas were chosen for discussion because they emerged in a natural and obvious way during the psychotherapeutic work. Their preeminence may be explained partially by the fact that each includes an unmistakable mixture of the basic instincts of sex and aggression. One area does not necessarily predominate over the others; rather, predominance fluctuates in the course of the work. These three areas are not meant to be exhaustive of the possibilities for acting out. This chapter is instead only an initial exploration of a topic unexplored elsewhere in the literature.

Sexual Fantasies

The issue of sexual fantasies is discussed less frequently than power or self-destructiveness, but sexual themes are ever present, though often nonverbally—in styles of dress, flirtatious mannerisms, and postures. On at least one occasion, however, sexual fantasies came to the fore and were acted out in a striking way. Four group members attended a male striptease show together. They reported it in the following session, amid laughter, a proud sense of achievement, and some embarrassment. It was an interesting group project, planned—outside meetings, of course—and successfully carried through despite the members' traumatic memories.

The organizer of this "outing" had previously seen a similar show; at that time she had undergone the trauma of being lifted onto the stage by a performer who proceeded to simulate a rape. The patient was so frozen by panic that she could not defend herself. Soon after she learned that her boyfriend had planned the whole thing as a practical joke. After that she experienced a counterphobic need to see the striptease again.

Other patients reported how they got back at men by doing to the strippers what men have done to them: sadistically scrutinizing the sexual endowment of the performers, making them feel self-conscious by shouting things like "shake it, baby."

Getting together to plan and to attend the show was a way of acting out a number of wishes: to exclude the therapists; to ventilate anger against men; and to do something sexual together.

Betty, who had once engaged in group sex with her lover and her best girlfriend, had organized this "outing." The lover knew about her attendance at the strip show and expressed special interest in having "the incest girls" over so he could "get to know them better.'' There were clear innuendos of possible group sex among the five. The male therapist commented on this, helping Betty realize she had been ignoring the shared though tacit sexual fantasy. Betty then recalled her intense suffering when, as a consequence of the group sex, she had lost her best friend. The sight of her lover having intercourse with the friend had made her feel excluded and unbearably jealous.

The naive "going along with the adventure" of the other group members stopped. They were able to state their unwillingness to "socialize" and clearly rejected any sexual involvement.

Power and Sadism

In an effort to avoid chaos, clinicians may artificially narrow their focus and, instead of realizing the kaleidoscopic complexity of the problem of incest, may adopt stereotypes in an effort to understand it. For instance, we initially referred to our patients simply as "victims," thus ignoring that they had also had the experience of feeling themselves powerful, the rulers of their homes.

They grew up learning to use their power stealthily within the family. This power may stem from various sources: control over family stability by maintaining the incest secret, including possible blackmailing of the abuser in order to remain father's "mistress" or "favorite"; assumption of a parenting role vis-à-vis parents and/or siblings; or identification with the abuser, who has sadistically used his power to get his way. Because the use of power is covert in these families, its behavioral manifestations in the group are often quite subtle. But they are nonetheless pervasive. Many instances, widely various, of acting out involving power and sadism have occurred during the group's life. We will describe only a few.

Karen is known among her friends as a master at intimidating people. She was also able to control the other group members, convincing them that the therapists, after they had brought up her possible relapse into drug abuse, were the enemy. She refused to establish eye contact with the therapists, sitting beside the male therapist with her back to him. In addition, she was furious with Anna, then a newcomer, who was cast in the role of her critic; Karen distorted Anna's comments, clearly responding to them as if she thought them callous, stupid, and irritating. Her anger at the therapists was thus displaced onto this new member. Later, Karen tried to approach Anna as they were leaving the building, but Anna did not hear her invitation to talk. Instead she continued toward her car, leaving Karen feeling victimized. The feelings elicited by this exchange were brought up in the next group meeting. Karen claimed Anna had behaved exactly like her father always had, expressing anger by remaining silent. Karen was projecting into Anna her own intimidating technique of ignoring other persons. Thus did the group learn that Karen's nonverbal intimidation replicated her father's behavior toward her.

By contrast, intimidation was exercised verbally by Betty. She cast the therapists in the role of being uncaring, arrogant, and stupid. She voiced serious doubts about our credentials and criticized our group techniques, caricaturing them as an old-fashioned, disreputable method of group treatment. She was joined by Wilma in claiming that "whatever good was coming out of the group came actually from the other group members, who were giving to each other, but nothing good was coming out of the therapists' interventions." This violent devaluation of the therapists culminated with Betty making calls to other agencies, inquiring about programs offering group therapy for incest victims. The patients were considering leaving as a group, to another agency, because they considered us unqualified to treat them.

During this bitter power struggle we felt cornered and controlled, fearful that anything we said would be construed as a sadistic attack on them. Communication was distorted to such an extent that at times it seemed impossible. We began doubting our ability to use our clinical skills in helping the group through this intense paranoid crisis.

Self-Destructiveness

These patients are prone to be self-destructive because of a need to expiate their guilt for incestuous activities. They may also use self-destructive behavior to attract attention and support.

Most of these patients struggle with feelings of love and hate toward their abuser. The guilt resulting from their awareness of this love can serve as a trigger for self-destructive behavior. Early in group formation, the necessity they feel to deny their love and instead parade their hate can intensify the internal self-reproaches of group members. The more vulnerable patients may become self-destructive, even to the point of attempting suicide.

Jane joined the group several months after its inception. Group members were still proclaiming their hatred for their incestuous partners, while Jane had currently a good relationship with her father. The group accused her of denying her anger. She was made to feel an outcast because she did not share the other members' hatred for their abusers. But in fact she had presented herself provocatively, as having already overcome her hatred, thereby eliciting the other members' criticism and ostracism. Unconsciously she was punishing herself for loving her father, and offered herself as the group scapegoat. This pattern of interaction continued for several sessions; her symptom of self-cutting was recurring in the meantime.

Wilma had considerable difficulty acknowledging her guilt verbally, but repeatedly acted in self-destructive ways. Following an argument with her boyfriend one dark evening, she defiantly hopped on her bicycle and rode a long distance on a winding country road. She was fully aware of the danger involved. Her

self-destructive tendencies attempted to deal with her unconscious
guilt, awareness of which she usually avoided by projecting it.
However, Wilma was gradually able to realize, with the group's
help, that whenever she "waged war against male enemies" she
was in fact struggling with internal guilt over being very much
like her father, who had sexually abused her.

Working Through

Working through is the solution to acting out. Several suc-
cessive steps can be described in the working through of acting
out: (1) the translation of acted out impulses into meaningful
interactions within the group, so that those interchanges may be
discussed and reflected upon; (2) the verbalization, by therapists
or patients, of the meaning of behaviors so they are made un-
derstandable; (3) the spread of self-understanding, with each patient translating someone else's words into the patient's own
language and realizing how the same behavior reappears in different contexts; (4) arrival at new and "advanced" reflections
of the repeated interactions of the patients with themselves, with
other group members, and with outsiders; and (5) new integrations
within the patient's mind that bring about new views of self and
others which may facilitate permanent behavioral changes.

Our patients have just begun to work through the issues
underlying their acting out. But some members are in relatively
advanced stages of working through their conflicts over sex,
power and sadism, and self-destructiveness.

Working Through of Sexual Conflicts

Sex as a matter to laugh about, or to avenge oneself with,
was followed months later by a need to work seriously on actual
difficulties these patients experienced in enjoying sex with their

partners. Wilma reported that she is anorgastic and feels very inadequate as a woman. Betty had a severe anxiety attack when a dentist put an anesthesia mask on her mouth; she had had flashbacks of her brother putting his hand over her mouth while sexually abusing her, so that nobody could hear her in their small and crowded home. Later she understood why she had difficulty accepting sex at night with her husband: the incestuous contacts had always occurred at night before she went to sleep. She reflected on this with her husband and helped him to better understand her avoidance of sex at night.

Patients' anger at themselves for their sexual responses was a particular problem when they had lubricated or had orgasms during incest. Some hated their bodies for having had a normal physiological response to sexual stimulation, in a situation where mentally they were rejecting the incestuous sexual partner. Their automatic, independent physical responses, regardless of the accompanying emotions of anger and revulsion, made them hate their own bodies.

Working Through of Power and Sadism

Karen's impulse to control the group had been gaining momentum for months. She would come late, leave early, and glower in silence, or have outbursts of anger at both therapists. Occasionally she gave evidence of her perception that the therapists were ignoring her, rather than vice versa. As noted above, examining her exchanges with Anna revealed that Karen was accusing Anna of abusing her with silent indifference, exactly as her father had. Karen's identification with the aggressor then became evident. In a private discussion precipitated by our frustration with this patient's controlling behavior, we diagnosed these unconscious defense mechanisms. Realizing that any intervention made by the male therapist would be rejected out of hand, we agreed that the female therapist would confront Karen with her intimidating behavior and the group with their fearful response. We hoped that this would start the working through process.

In the next session, Karen continued her angry, controlling behavior. As we attempted to interact with her, she furiously arose to leave the room. The female therapist then told Karen that she was intimidating everyone with her behavior. Karen halted, her hand on the doorknob. The word intimidation had brought an expression of astonishment to her face. Just as Karen hesitated at the door, before leaving silently, there was a remarkable release of tension in the room. As she left, everyone commented, for the first time ever, how intimidated they had been by her. Group members agreed with the therapist's confrontation and elaborated on it with a noncritical and understanding attitude. The matter-of-fact tone of the therapist's confrontation was serving them as a model.

The following sessions were not characterized by an atmosphere of intimidation. Initially Karen participated silently. She said she would now be able to remain through entire sessions, adding, ''I shall eventually be able to talk with you but right now do not talk to me, because I may not yet be able to take it.'' Although her words were addressed to both therapists, nonverbal indications made clear that she was talking primarily to the male therapist. The other members accepted and supported Karen without fearing her; no longer were they under her control.

Working Through Self-Destructiveness

Self-destructiveness is an expression of self-hatred. These patients hate themselves because they reproach themselves for their sexual activities with family members and for being like their abusers.

Betty deprived herself of many things she could easily afford. Whenever she tried to buy herself something, she felt undeserving and a panic attack would ensue. Gradually she began to connect these reactions with her past: she revealed that her brothers had paid her to participate in sex with them. Sometimes they charged admission to neighborhood children to see her do an explicit striptease. Betty had also become friendly with several prostitutes who lived next door to her. In this context, having money available to her reminded her that she had been paid for sex. As she shared these details of her past with the group, Betty realized that her inability to buy things for herself was related to self-hatred inspired by her feeling that she had sold her body. Once she realized this, Betty was able to interpret to herself the meaning of her conflict over buying herself things, to the extent that from then on she could sense incipient anxiety attacks and nip them in the bud.

Wilma went through the three major forms of acting out—sexual, sadistic, and self-destructive—when she caught herself in a flirtation with a younger man. She wished to seduce him as a way of overcoming her doubts about herself as a woman. But when she realized she was attempting with this man what her father had done with her, she hated herself for being "like her father," her abuser. She was indeed using a young man to bolster her self-esteem and, by showering him with special attention from a mature woman, was making him feel important; her becoming the source of his self-esteem gave her leverage with which to dominate him. But the more this young man seemed interested in her, making her feel the center of his universe, the better she felt about herself. Later on, however, her self-hatred for psychologically abusing this young man increased to the point of her becoming intensely depressed and unable to concentrate at work for a few days. Some evenings Wilma needed to get drunk to feel better about herself, obliterating her preoccupation with the young man; later on she would catch herself driving drunk and recklessly, sometimes even causing her neighbors to be concerned for her. Although it was not really the case, Wilma felt as if she were planning to abuse a child, just as her father had.

In the group we interpreted her self-hatred as anger at the part of herself that was like her father, and explained her suicidal fantasies as a wish to rid herself of "the abuser within her." In response she cried, saying that she did not want to go on living.

The fear of being like the hated abuser is a common concern of incest victims. It is peculiarly combined—because of identification with the aggressor—with struggles to overcome an unbearable guilt for having committed the heinous act. Wilma was playing out this drama in the group, striving to expiate her own guilt and be pardoned, at the same time she implicitly asked forgiveness for her abuser, whose internal tragedy she shared. Since such tragedy is well known to incest victims, the group members were able to empathize with Wilma, as no other group could. They helped Wilma forgive herself, through understanding her narcissistic needs, her unfulfilled sexual wishes, and her need to be domineering with persons she cares for. The group members succeeded in getting Wilma to understand herself. As soon as she stopped being so devastatingly harsh in judging herself, she was able to put herself in her father's shoes and diminish her condemnation of him. The group's love for Wilma helped her to forgive.

Feeling loved usually increases self-esteem, but this is particularly so during incestuous experiences—for both parties. The abuser uses the victim's admiration, fear, and love to bolster low self-esteem. Thus the victim exercises a kind of mothering function toward the abuser. Wilma had cast her young man in this same nurturant role. Her groupmates supported her by acknowledging and "legitimating" these narcissistic exchanges between her and the young man, and by partially meeting her needs to feel good about herself.

The working through process was expanded later when Wilma realized the displacement: that she planned to meet with

the young man whenever she felt frustrated either by her individual psychotherapist, by the group male therapist, or by her
age-appropriate boyfriend. Through realizing this displacement
she understood a deeper meaning of her acting out, that she was
casting her young man in a nurturant role comparable to the
functions she had herself assumed as a child toward her lonely,
deprived, and insecure father. She used her own words to describe
her realization that she was repeating in different contexts her
father's "typical behaviors."

Discussion

Acting out, a special resistance to exploratory psychotherapeutic work, may occur during treatment for a variety of psychopathological conditions. It is therefore impossible to lay down
a set of general rules for its management. Instead, a case-by-case
assessment is necessary. Sometimes the therapists must directly
limit acting out (Ormont, 1969; Borriello, 1973, 1979), as when
the behaviors are seriously self-destructive, are illegal, or severely
curtail the psychotherapeutic work. But some forms of acting
out, as we have noted, have an adaptive connotation and may be
therapeutically productive as the "practicing" of new behaviors
(Yalom, 1975).

The therapists' theoretical model guides their approach to
acting out. The existential model, for instance, advocates practicing new behaviors in every "new encounter" (Yalom, 1975).
Behavioral modification uses techniques of punishment and re-
ward to modify acting out. The psychoanalytic model strives to
develop an understanding of the patient's actions. "Complete"
working through of acting out is seldom attainable. Usually during
psychotherapy, acting out behavior will alternate with periods of
reflection and new insight.

Acting out is inevitable in the treatment of these patients

because taking action is essential in mastering traumatic experiences. Further, acting is a style of relating within their families of origin. Because of this, working through will not stop acting out but will gradually modify it. Talking about their experiences may be especially difficult for these adult patients because of their belief in the omnipotence of words—as if talking about the experience were the same as reliving it.

Intense countertransference, vividly experienced, is a major therapist response to these patients' actions. Cotherapy is helpful in working through these feelings in the therapists as it is possible to think together about the messages expressed by acting out. Each patient can be helped to understand the unconscious communication of the acting out behavior. The assistance of group members in achieving this goal is clearly advantageous. Developing the patients' willingness to examine the meanng of the acting out behavior is the real product of effective psychotherapeutic work.

Thus, a natural proclivity for acting out is not a contraindication for group psychotherapy with these patients. Realizing that the patient is attempting to communicate meaningful unconscious material may focus the work more sharply, facilitating the translation of actions into words.

Chapter 4

Survival of the Self in Incest Victims

The concept of the self and its clinical applications are central to contemporary psychoanalytic theory and practice. In reference to their enormous difficulties in developing an integrated, cohesive sense of self, victims of incest are frequently called survivors. This chapter describes their struggles for psychological survival.

The Concepts of Self and Self-Representation

The *self* is a descriptive, experiential term referring to the whole person, including both mind and body. This commonsense concept contrasts the individual with others, whom we call "objects" (McDonald, 1981). It is a social psychological concept formed at the boundaries between the person and the others. It is a mixture of the proactive expressions of the emergent individual searching for validation by others and by their responses. The development of the self is a dynamic, life-long process; the self constantly changes throughout the life cycle. An environment that fits the individual's needs has a healing effect on the damaged self. Thus the self is an evolving entity formed by the individual's active striving for self-expression, plus the varying responses from the environment. Threats against the self create a fear of losing it, while its validation by others enhances self-esteem and self-survival. "Human beings," writes Gabriel Garcia Marquez (1985), "are not born once and for all, the day their mothers deliver them, but life again and again forces them to give birth to themselves" (p. 227).

Self-representation is a related concept, "a metapsychological concept" referring to the "unconscious, preconscious, and conscious endopsychic representations of the bodily and mental self in the system ego" (Jacobson, 1964, p. 19). McDonald (1981) stresses that self-representation portrays the person as conceived by himself or herself—both consciously and unconsciously. McDonald also commented that when "self" is used what is often really meant is "self-representation." This careless use has gained common acceptance. Some noted theoreticians use the terms interchangeably, with the result of wide-spread confusion.

Winnicott (1960) brought the concept of the self to a meaningful clinical application when he wrote about ego distortions in terms of true and false self. He described the drama of persons who, though successful in their lives, had the feeling of "not yet having started to exist." He conceived of the false self as defending the true self by hiding and protecting it and constantly searching for conditions in which it could come into its own. He described the false self as built on identifications that promote its organization, an organization of polite and mannered social attitudes, of not wearing one's heart on one's sleeve," thus gaining the individual a place in society that could never have been attained by the true self alone.

Greenberg and Mitchell (1983) write that Winnicott depicts "the continually hazardous struggle of the self for an individuated existence which at the same time allows for intimate contact with others'' (p. 190). For Winnicott, lack of contact with others and total accessibility to them pose equally grave dangers to the self. The state of devotion that enables the mother to offer herself willingly as an attentive medium for her baby's growth he characterized as a state of "primary maternal preoccupation" (p. 191).

The mother provides experiences which enable the incipient self of the infant to emerge. The latter begins life in a state of "unintegration," with scattered and diffused bits and pieces of experience. The infant's organization of his own experience is preceded by and draws upon the mother's organized perceptions of him. The mother provides a "holding environment" within which the infant is contained and experienced. [p. 191]

Viewing the interpersonal world of the infant from a psychoanalytic developmental perspective yields several senses of the self: an emergent self, a core self, a subjective self, and a verbal self (Stern, 1985). Each of these selves emerges during a different type of relatedness with the others. None proceeds through rigid phases or stages; rather, each has an ebb and flow of growth, intermingling with the other selves in different outbursts of development. The coordinated, one-track growth assumed by other developmental theories has no place here. Stern sums up the views of Balint, Klein, Sullivan, Fairbairn, and Guntrip when he states that "human social relatedness is present from birth, it exists for its own sake, is of a definable nature, and does not lean upon physiological need states" (p. 44). He adds that attachment theorists such as Bowlby have elaborated this view and supported it with objective data. Stern emphasizes that "the infant's *direct* social experience is the . . . central focus of concern in the views of the British object relations school and the American parallel schools which have also enhanced human social relatedness as present from birth" (p. 44).

Jacobson (1971) studied depersonalization as a "disturbance in a person's relation with his own self," not limited to psychotics but observable also in normal persons after trauma. It reflects "a split between two opposing self-representations" that conflict within the ego, between an acceptable part and another part rejected because it represents "identifications with a degraded object image" (p. 147). Depersonalization is an experience pertaining to the representation of both the physical and the mental self. The person complains that certain parts of the body do not feel as if they belong to him, or there is a feeling of unreality of the self, of being "outside of the self . . . as a detached spectator who is observing another person's performance" (pp. 137–138).

Kohut (1977) questioned the basic viewpoint of the psychoanalytic dual instinct theory, asserting—like Fairbairn (1952) before him—that the human being is primarily seeking objects as opposed to striving for the gratification of impulses. Aggression is not instinctive but secondary to frustrations in the interactions with objects. For Kohut (1977), the "experiencing self" is an independent "center of initiative" that has aims, intentions, and plans; is the agent of its own actions; and assumes responsibility for its decisions, providing feelings of continuity and sameness across the years. Thus normal emotional development culminates in the consolidation of a fully coherent self that Kohut (1984) defines "in terms of structural . . . completeness . . . achieved . . . when an energic continuum in the center of the personality has been established and the unfolding of a productive life has thus become a realizable possibility" (p. 7). Kohut (1984) sees the structural self as nothing more than "an uninterrupted tension arch from basic ambitions, via basic talents and skills, toward basic ideals. This tension arch is the dynamic essence of the complete nondefective self" (pp. 4–5). The realization of our lives occurs within a responsive self-object milieu necessary for the sustenance of human life. For Kohut, "normal psychological development does not require the self's relinquishment of self-objects'' (p. 47); rather ''health consists in the ability to identify and seek out appropriate self-objects'' available in the surroundings and ''to be sustained by them'' (p. 77). In the opinion of Horwitz (1984), the advantages of the superordinate concept of the self may be to present

> a concept of experiential self . . . that contains both conscious and unconscious elements, organizes one's primary identity as well as hidden selves and subselves, and provides a sense of continuity and stability. . . . In addition, to define the self as the central experiential agent and integrator of diverse identities suggests that the ego's system functions are subordinate to a concept of self. I believe it may best be viewed as the superordinate organizing structure for the tripartite elements of the mind. [pp. 524, 527]

Psychopathology of the Self

The pathology of the self is contingent on either a lack of endorsement by the infant's significant others or on an absence of ''environmental fit'' with the child's needs. If the child is used as a narcissistic extension of the parents, this may curtail or impinge on the development of the child's self. When injuries to the incipient self occur early and are later reinforced, the self has difficulty surviving. Fortunately, however, later validations of the self by significant others are an aid to survival, and environments that fit the needs of the self may foster the healing of the damaged self.

The literature reports a variety of self pathology. Fairbairn (1940) described the schizoid factors in the personality as a result of an unintegrated or noncohesive self, insisting that ''it is a common finding to observe the basically schizoid nature displayed by patients who present themselves as psychoneurotic''

(p. 5). He described depersonalization and derealization, minor disturbances of the sense of reality (e.g., feelings of artificiality, the experience of déjà vu), and other dissociative phenomena such as fugues and dual or multiple personality. Fairbairn developed a clinically useful concept of fragmented, hidden subselves containing important but unintegrated elements of the personality.

When Winnicott (1960) described the true self and the false self and their interrelations, he distinguished several degrees of false self. These ranged "from the healthy polite aspect of the self to the truly split-off compliant false self" (p. 150). Some patients experience the struggle between the true and the false self as a confusion about their own identity; they feel they don't know who they really are or have a vague sense of acting like impostors.

Kohut (1968) described the narcissistic personality disorders as resulting from a deficit of validation of the self by significant others. He described low self-esteem, typical narcissistic transferences such as mirroring or idealization of the object, and styles of interaction with objects whereby there is a loss of boundary between self and object so that objects are treated as extensions of the self and acknowledged only insofar as they provide gratifications of grandiose, narcissistic self-needs. At times narcissistic low self-esteem reaches the point of becoming the individual's negative identity, and the person sees only negative attitudes as characterizing the self. In Kohut's summary of a successful analysis (1984), he states that the treatment will be "successful because . . . an analysand was able to reactivate, in a self-object transference, the needs of a self that had been thwarted in childhood. . . . The essence of the psychoanalytic cure resides in the patient's newly acquired ability to (1) identify and seek out appropriate self-objects . . . as they present themselves in his realistic surroundings, and (2) to be sustained by them" (p. 77).

Bauman (1981) relates the true self/false self hypothesis to the mirroring concept:

When mirroring lacks sufficient *vitality* and *enthusiasm*, the
child may attempt to regain "a lost sense of aliveness" by
resorting to any available means of stimulating him. The stimulation can be in the form of fantasy formation, hyperactivity,
lonely masturbation, various physical symptoms. . . . A good
enough mother must meet the infant's gesture, mirror it, give
it life and meaning. Then a true self begins to have life. [p.
463]

Bauman also explains that affirming or nonaffirming environmental and bodily experiences contribute to body image as well
as self-image. Altering the body image may cause hypochondriacal anxieties and distortions in one's bodily perceptions. Anorexia nervosa has been described as connected with pathology
of the self, insofar as it is based on a quasi-delusional distortion
of the patient's perception of his or her own body image.

In Kohut's *Analysis of the Self* (1971) he states: "Viewed
metapsychologically the deeply frightening feelings of fragmentation and deadness which the child experiences are a manifestation of the fact that, in the absence of the narcissistically
invested self-object, the cathexis is withdrawn from a cohesively
experienced self and regressive fragmentation and hypochondriacal tensions now threaten the child" (p. 99). Further, "an
analogy between the patient's present hypochondriacal concerns
and the vague health worries of a lonely child who feels unprotected and threatened can be drawn, facilitating the patient's grasp
of the deeper meaning of his present condition as well as of its
genetic roots" (p. 137).

Kohut (1971) considered hypochondriasis a response to nar-
cissitic transferences:

The preoccupation with one's own body which occurs regularly
in physical illness is a manifestation of increased narcissism. . . .
In psychotic or prepsychotic hypochondriasis . . . , individual

body parts, or isolated physical or mental functions, become isolated and hypercathected. . . . If a person with strong pre-narcissistic fixations becomes physically ill, then the increase in body narcissism which accompanies the physical illness may bring about a further regression toward a stage of beginning body-self fragmentation and, instead of experiencing whole-some self-concern, the person will react with hypochondriacal anxiety. [p. 215]

This anxiety he explained as follows: "The hypercathexis of isolated mental functions and mechanisms . . . , which occurs after fragmentation of the mental self, is a frequent complement to the physical hypochondriasis of early stages of psychotic regression and is thus experienced analogous to psychological hypochondriasis (i.e., for example, rationalized as worry over the loss of one's intellect, fear of insanity, and the like)" (pp. 216–217).

Incest and Psychopathology of the Self

Incest, that extreme assault on the self, ignores the needs of the child while those of the adult predominate. The child is used to gratify the abuser's urges. Generational boundaries are not observed, thus ignoring the child's need for a structure within which to develop a clear and integrated sense of self. The result can be an extremely confused self-image.

When a child discloses incest, the confidant may frequently reinforce, wittingly or not, the victim's debased self-image. The confidant may exhibit disbelief or may blame the child for dis-rupting the family. When this happens, the child may withdraw from social contacts, recant the accusation, suffer a drop in school performance, or act out in a self-destructive manner.

While conduct disorders may be the childhood consequences

of the incest trauma, its adult effects vary considerably. In order to present a socially acceptable front to the world at large, many incest victims develop a false self. Others have a confused sense of who they are. Many suffer low self-esteem because positive reinforcement to the self was denied to them by significant others. In some cases a negative identity may be fostered by an excess of negative feedback. Some incest victims develop noncohesive, fragmented selves and suffer dissociative states of consciousness in an attempt to protect the parts of themselves which they experience as good. Many victims develop narcissistic personality traits such as self-centeredness and a lack of consideration for the emotional needs of others. The distortions of body image that underlie anorexia nervosa may also be expressions of psychopathology of the self.

One patient seen in consultation suffered from multiple personality; when discussing the incest, she became the little girl who had been violated and talked in partial sentences similar to the baby talk of a small child. She was unable to take care of herself in basic ways (e.g., she could not use the kitchen stove safely despite years of experience as a homemaker). At other times she was completely unaware of having behaved like a little girl, being unable to recall interactions while in the childlike state of mind. The part of her that had been sexually abused had not been integrated with her self-image as an adult woman.

One group member began therapy with four places of residence: her own apartment, her best girlfriend's home (where she spent most of her evenings), and the condominiums of two different boyfriends where she alternately spent her nights. These multiple residences reflected her disconnected, contradictory self-perceptions as the independent individual she aspired to be, a dependent child taken care of by different grownups, or a young adolescent woman in love.

One young woman came to us in search of help. She was an incest victim who suffered from a dramatic struggle between her false self and her true self. "I don't know who I am," she said, "since I grew up trying to please everybody. I don't know what I myself really want." She had been involved in several incestuous relationships, as if sexual contact were the only way to get and give affection, in spite of the tremendous shame that ensued. Her false self was also a way to hide her unconscious identification with her mother, whom she disliked. She explained that there were two parts of her—a "people-pleaser" and her real self.

A young female patient had a hypochondriacal preoccupation with the skin of her face. She suffered from relatively mild acne but was convinced her face was seriously disfigured. She developed face-washing rituals and phobic avoidance of substances she thought might affect her skin; she acted as if the mere *idea* of ingesting them would do her further damage. Her worries were so intense that she wished for an immediate, magical cure through medication; when the condition of her skin did not improve, she gave up hope entirely. On several occasions she made serious suicidal attempts requiring psychiatric hospitalization. The patient lived on an emotional roller coaster: high points came when she thought a clear somatic diagnosis was established or a new drug for acne was prescribed; low points occurred with lack of daily improvement of her skin, which she examined with a magnifying mirror, or when any doubts were expressed that her condition was only physical. Treaters were accordingly idealized or vilified. New treaters could usually ride on the crest of some new hope for a while. She idealized them until they failed to deliver on alleged promises, then vilified and devalued them as ignorant liars or mean, controlling individuals.

This patient's preoccupation with her face began shortly after her mother became psychotic and required hospitalization. The patient felt then that everybody looked at her during Sunday church services, as if wondering how much she resembled her mother. The patient developed the conviction that no young man in her small community would ever consider marrying her, for fear that like her mother she would become psychotic. Her mother's insanity made the patient feel that she had "lost face." She felt oppressed by her mother's social image, and thought being like her mother a disgrace. It was then she started over-valuing her facial appearance.

As the oldest daughter in a large family, the patient was expected to share child-rearing and homemaking responsibilities with her mother. Her family circumstances thus pushed her into becoming a mother surrogate. As her mother became psychiatrically ill, the patient had to assume more and more of the maternal functions in the household. In the midst of this situation, her mother accused her of having an affair with her father. The patient responded by trying to hide her closeness to her father; for instance, when riding with her father, she would move to the back seat of the car as they approached home. She was sexually aroused by pornographic magazines containing sadistic material such as bloody scenes of the murder of a woman killed by her rival. Murderous wishes against her mother were not disguised but generated a combination of sexual arousal, intense guilt, and shame. The patient was convinced that God was punishing her for being "so mean." The ultimate penalty would be for her to become a replica of her mother, "losing face" just like her. The patient experienced envy and jealousy of women she perceived as happier and more attractive than she, only to have the aware-ness that she was as jealous as her mother, which induced suicidal fury in her. The face-washing rituals had several condensed un-conscious meanings: washing away the blood like Lady Macbeth; expiating guilt through the torture involved in such rituals, which included compulsively asking forced witnesses whether she had washed her face enough.

The family atmosphere was incestuous (i.e., the patient had been pushed into assuming a maternal role in the family, and she treasured her special place with her father). However, the patient did not recall having had sexual contact with her father. Instead she was quite open about her attraction to one of her brothers, whom she found more attractive than most other men; frequently they lay naked together in bed. The patient needed to localize her anxiety in her skin, denying her psychiatric condition. She rejected the part of herself that identified with her mother. Regression to body/self fragmentation had occurred, with the patient attempting to undo her partial maternal identification.

Some of these patients have a history of both incest and anorexia nervosa, both of which are hidden, or secret, psychopathological conditions. The psychopathology of the self underlying anorexia represents the "relationship between the bodily sense of self and the psychic self" (Rizzuto, Peterson, and Reed, 1981, p. 474). Accordingly, anorexics feel "that their parents can acknowledge only their bodily presence" (p. 474) and discount their yearning for recognition of the psychic self. One anorexic woman we interviewed quite characteristically saw herself as fat, despite her looking like a model; she starves herself and frequently overexercises. The abuser who manipulated her into an incestuous liaison did so by insisting that sexual activities would make her perspire profusely and help her lose weight. Her self-image was damaged before the incest, in that she already believed she was obese. Her abuser reinforced this body image to obtain her consent and provided a possible solution to her imagined weight problem; simultaneously, he communicated that he found her physically attractive.

Betty, one of the original seven group members, has an extremely low self-image. One sense of herself is as a potential prostitute, thief, liar, and exploiter, despite many assets such as her resumption of formal education in middle age, relatively stable intimate relationships and skills in managing her family budget. She survived an early impoverished background by becoming streetwise and learning useful skills. These adaptive aspects, however, are superseded by an unrelenting depreciation of herself.

Since many incest victims have negative identities on this order, placement in a homogeneous group formed only of incest victims may implicitly reinforce them in this—they may see themselves as belonging to a group of "misfits." This secondary negative identity may become antitherapeutic through rewarding a sense of being a social outcast. Incest victims may view improvement as a threat, something that would deprive them of their sense of belonging to a "special group" and the advantages of such membership (e.g., belonging to a group of outcasts may give them an inflated sense of entitlement to be rageful which may be difficult to relinquish).

Psychopathology of the Self and Life Changes

Acute self pathology is likely to erupt when important life changes occur. Dramatic body changes as well as new familial and social roles may significantly alter the self-images of incest victims.

Body Changes

Many of our patients have had serious physical illnesses, several of a life-threatening nature. Because their bodies had repeatedly let them down, two of these patients had the firm conviction they would die at a young age. They saw themselves as damaged and predestined to physical suffering and early death. Betty had a view of her body as damaged and was pessimistically convinced that she would die young because of a chronic heart condition. When at one point her condition became acute, the group and her individual psychotherapist challenged Betty's sense of hopelessness, encouraging her to avail herself of new treatment techniques. She received a complete modern treatment, despite her protest over expenses and other inconveniences, and recovered. Following this illness, she lightheartedly informed the group that she was revising her life plans because obviously she would not die soon but likely had many years ahead of her. Her view of herself had changed, overturning her belief that she was cursed to die young in punishment for her "sins."

Two of our patients required psychiatric treatment after having undergone hysterectomies. Although emotional disturbance in response to hysterectomy is not unusual, these patients suffered mental consequences that were striking in their intensity and severity. They required hospitalization, one for severe depression and drug addiction, another for a psychotic reaction. In both cases, incest was disclosed for the first time during their hospitalizations. Both had fantasies they were being punished for their incest experience by the loss of their reproductive organs.

Becoming pregnant had raised in all these patients the fear of delivering children they would be unable to love, protect, and nurture. On the one hand they feared having a boy they would be unable to love because he was male, who would be an undesirable product of their defective bodies, while on the other they imagined female infants as weak and vulnerable, and pictured themselves as unable to protect them. They believed their daughters doomed to repeat their own histories. Unwanted pregnancies play a special role in these women's view of themselves. Several know their mothers did not desire a child when they were conceived; one was told by her mother that she had attempted to abort her. Their common view of themselves as unwanted is central to their self-images.

When Wilma was an adolescent, she was impregnated by her father and then forced by him to have an abortion, which she resented. The fact that her baby was not wanted made her feel unwanted herself, mainly in consequence of the incest experience. Since Wilma did not produce a desirable child, the development of a sense of herself as a woman was thwarted. Shortly thereafter, she left home prematurely and took up a self-destructive life-style that led ultimately to her first psychiatric hospitalization.

Family Role Changes

Leaving home. Many of these patients have left their parents' homes abruptly, marrying impulsively or going to college without their financial assistance. Family dynamics such as the father's jealousy and their status as parenting children exerted pressure on them to stay within the family or run away without warning. Unable to separate gradually, several jumped into a relationship with the first available man, marrying him prematurely, going from parents to husbands treated as self-objects. They did not see themselves as capable of functioning independently and so substituted reliance on a spouse for dependency on their families of origin.

Marriage. Although the dependency needs of these patients led to impulsive marriages, their choice of spouse was frequently determined by masochistic submissiveness caused by self-depreciation and an unconscious search for punishment. Several group members who married early in order to leave home chose husbands who were physically abusive, alcoholic, and verbally demeaning. Martha deliberately chose her first husband as a means of leaving her father's house. Her spousal choice, however, revealed her perception of herself as deserving of mistreatment; shortly after the wedding, her husband began beating her and she then became aware of his alcoholism. Within a year they were divorced. Martha's second husband is much more caring and nurturant, but objects to the inconvenience her treatment causes him. If she is to come to treatment, Martha needs his help financially and with baby-sitting their children. Wishing to avoid asking for help altogether, Martha finds it difficult to ask her husband for the necessary assistance; instead she is extremely sensitive to his natural but really rather minimal objections to these inconveniences. She sees herself as once again victimized and reacts fearfully to her husband, as if he were abusive. The group members questioned Martha's perception of herself, helping her recognize her fearful distortion and encouraging her to assert herself. Martha reacted by saying she did not want to get into violent arguments. The therapists suggested that she was confusing aggression with self-assertion, as if it were impossible to negotiate without violence. Martha said that in her family of origin the only way to resolve disputes was through violence.

Children's growth. These patients have difficulties letting their children individuate and separate. They tend instead to treat them as narcissistic extensions of themselves, not as individuals in their own right. Boundaries between mother and child are thus frequently blurred in these mothers' minds.

The growth of daughters arouses fears about their vulnerability and their need for maternal protection. The patients frequently tried to be better mothers than their own by teaching their daughters how to defend themselves against possible sexual abuse. For instance, Karen spoke to the group about her apprehension in regard to her daugher's visiting her grandfather, who had been Karen's childhood abuser; she did not trust his behavior when alone with his granddaughter. The group members inquired if Karen had educated her daughter about how to protect herself. Ingrid, who also had a young daughter, provided Karen information about programs designed to educate children about sexual abuse. By allowing their daughters to grow beyond themselves and become capable of protecting themselves, these mothers were fostering their daughters' individuation. At the same time, however, they were projecting their own internal child into their daughters and promoting their own feelings.

Sometimes the goal of helping daughters grow gets mixed up with fears about the daughters' personal interests. That was the case with Anna, who struggled frequently with her tendency to make her own problems also her daughter's, particularly with regard to Anna's wish to cut off all relations with her mother. This wish conflicted with her daughter's interest in getting to know her maternal grandmother. Anna partly expected her daughter to take her side against her mother, blaming her for Anna's victimization and therefore severing all relations with her.

As noted above, these women have fears concerning their ability to mother a male child. These fears interfere with their capacity for adequate mothering, especially in regard to their sons' developing sexuality. Anna supports the growth of her son's absorbing asexual interests, which tend to confine him to a lonely role; she also overreacts to his minor physical ailments, emphasizing her view of him as weak and sick. Her view of him was most sharply stated when Wilma shared details of a lover who was the same age as Anna's son. As the lover was described in increasingly sexual terms, Anna emphasized her son's innocence.

Betty too denied her son's adulthood. She gave him a substantial monthly allowance, despite his capacity to support himself. The secret, clandestine atmosphere of these financial transactions was filled with erotic overtones. Both concealed the arrangement from Betty's husband. Although she complained of the financial burden, she reinforced her son's dependency and created an illicit family liaison, one comparable to that of another patient and a brother who abused her. By acting as if her son were her sibling, Betty was collapsing the generational boundaries between them.

Financial changes. Anna's attitude regarding money changed considerably, from an initial passive stance of feeling impoverished and victimized to a more active approach toward becoming economically confident. For most of her childhood her mother had struggled to support the family, but they never had enough money; the little that was available was managed chaotically. Anna describes the early years of her marriage as financially strained. Early in treatment the cost of her psychotherapy became an issue. With much difficulty, she communicated to her husband her distress over family finances. The resulting changes included the construction of a family budget and Anna's finding employment to pay for her treatment. Instead of viewing herself as financially beleaguered and deprived, she now took pride in her ability to earn and manage money. She now sees herself as an agent in solving her problems, rather than as the victim of someone else's financial mismanagement.

Social changes. Social changes such as moving to a new neighborhood or school, job promotions, new religious affiliations, and court appearances may all have the power to significantly affect self-images. For instance, when as a child Betty moved from a poor neighborhood to one in a wealthy section of town, she developed a tendency to comply with her classmates by hiding her family chaos and streetwise demeanor, so that she would appear as privileged and serene as her classmates. However, this made her feel like an impostor, whose unveiling would result in ostracism. Thus her false self allowed her to be accepted in the new neighborhood.

A deficit of appropriate approval from their parents leaves these women yearning for recognition of their assets by other authority figures. For instance, Wilma was pleased at receiving an award at work for seniority and longevity. Yet being recognized is so infrequent for her that initially she planned not to claim the award. A number of group members highly value their religious affiliations because they appreciate the community support and implicit godly approval as a reinforcement of their self-worth.

When Wilma's father began to abuse Wilma's sister, Wilma decided to report his behavior to the authorities. She derived satisfaction from making this public revelation but was quite disappointed when his sentence consisted of probation with no imprisonment. By taking the matter to court, Wilma dramatically severed her ties with her family. Following the court proceedings she began to see herself as an active and powerful person who no longer experienced herself as passively victimized. From then on her behavior became defiant and rebellious rather than compliant.

Karen too has been involved in court proceedings, but of a different nature. She has been convicted of crimes related to her forging of checks. Ashamed of her illegal activity, she views herself as despicable, as even more lowly and worthless than before. Paradoxically, however, Karen's self-defeat is transformed in her mind into a powerful weapon with which to humiliate her socially prominent family.

Both these patients, though ashamed of themselves, have obtained satisfaction from besmirching their families' reputations. They felt powerful particularly in being able to damage the reputations of their fathers.

The self in groups. Horwitz (1984) selects three group functions that influence or modify the self: (1) mirroring; (2) peer relationships, particularly partnering; and (3) a sense of belonging. Horwitz uses the term *mirroring* to "include both the responses that the individual *receives* from others and the reactions to others that he or she *transmits* to them . . . sometimes the individual looks into the mirror others hold up to him, and at other times he or she may become the mirror itself" (p. 530). He comments that the dual mirroring functions in a group are "prime factors in uncovering and exposing 'hidden parts' of the self. These unintegrated self-representations are part of the dynamic unconscious that, nevertheless, influence an individual's character style, contribute to symptoms, and modify overt behavior. They determine one's sense of cohesiveness and self-esteem as well as feelings of acceptability and genuineness" (p. 530). Horwitz conceives the peer relatedness and partnering, or interrelationships among group members, as unique features of groups that offer unusual opportunities for therapeutic influence." Bacal (1983) described such a "partnering transference" as an expression of "the wish for a relationship characterized by equality and mutuality. Developmentally, it is most prominent in adolescents when they relate to a buddy or intimate confidant, and it "represents a significant step towards liberation from familial ties" (cited in Horwitz, 1984, p. 533). Finally, Horwitz comments on "the sense of belonging to a group offering a 'supportive aspect' for being valued, found needed and desirable by others, and being capable of contributing to others," which leads to "a considerable rise in self-esteem" (p. 535).

In contrast to this description of what happens to the self in small groups, a completely different situation occurs in large groups, as observed during the A. K. Rice Institute Group Relations Conferences. In large groups participants feel "drowned" in a collective anonymity; "there are too many of them to create the interindividual relationships that allow them to feel that they exist" (Anzieu, 1984, p. 73). The difficulties in knowing others and interacting with them in a large group include the danger of losing one's own self. The others become a mirror that reflects nothing. Face-to-face relationships are impossible. The large group has no unity and "undergoes a temporary experience of depersonalization"; participants often experience the unconscious fantasy of breaking apart, "an archaic anxiety that the personality will fragment" (Anzieu, 1984, p. 74). According to Anzieu's summary of Turquet's views (1974), there occurs as compensation an anxious search for bonds with one's neighbors.

Self-Image Improvement During Group Psychotherapy for Incest

A *sense of belonging* to a group has significant therapeutic value that may lead to improvement in patients' self-images. Horwitz (1984) described how group members supply specific self needs such as mirroring and idealization, being freer than the therapists to express empathic responses.

During one group session with these incest victims, one member professed her love for the others, enumerating each member by name except one. No comment was made then about the omission, but in a later session the therapists wondered if the anger and sadness being expressed by the omitted member could be related to her having been left off that list. At that point Marge, usually a woman of few words and a newcomer who had stayed relatively marginal to the group, intervened to confirm and elaborate the therapists' observation. She said that she noted how hurtful the omission had been for the slighted patient. Other members expressed admiration for Marge's sensitivity and good memory, making her feel pleased with herself as a valued group member.

Partnering in a group is another way self-image is improved. It "reflects a healthy wish for a mature, reciprocal relationship with another person," like adolescent confidants (Horwitz, 1984, p. 533). Examples of sibling transference were discussed in chapter 2. Partnering may reflect a tendency to idealize groupmates as "best friends" but is usually based on the active exchange of experiences and support. For instance, when Wilma was involved in an anxiety-ridden love affair and was full of self-doubt and self-recriminations, Betty was the only group member to clearly support her. The others criticized and opposed Wilma's emotional involvement. Betty's empathic capacity allowed her to put herself in Wilma's place and understand her dilemma.

In more general terms, these group members supported each other in reviewing their sexual lives. One by one, they revealed dissatisfaction with themselves and with their partners. They discussed the matter frequently during group meetings, taking risks to share problems in this painful area. Three of these patients eventually decided to seek more extensive change by obtaining supplementary sex therapy with the active collaboration of their sexual partners.

In *mirroring* the members figuratively hold up a mirror so

that one patient can look into it. Mirroring also involves the process by which each member becomes a mirror to the others (Horwitz, 1984).

Soon after the beginning of the group, Wilma's response to stressful interactions was to withdraw, look at her hands, nervously jiggle her feet, and say nothing. A pattern developed whereby Wilma became involved with other group members in a tug-of-war over whether she would speak. With the therapists' help, the members learned to identify the presence of Wilma's "pouting self" (of which she was unaware) as indicative of her suffering. After that the tug-of-war stopped occurring, as members voiced their perception that Wilma was distressed: "You are so quiet today, what is troubling you?" The mirroring function of the other group members expanded Wilma's self-awareness so that she was able to integrate the suffering side of herself she had previously denied. She was then able to address her distress more genuinely and productively.

Presenting a facade of self-sufficiency, Wilma had repeatedly denied she needed mothering from anyone. But as the group began to acknowledge their own unfulfilled yearnings for comfort from their mothers, Wilma panicked. Frantic, she demanded contact with a host of nurturing persons outside the group, desperately substituting one for another. The pretense, intended as much for herself as for others, was that she was dependent on no one in particular but was self-sufficiently managing a list of emotional supporters. As her dependency needs intensified, the number of frantic contacts increased: she called her individual psychotherapist late at night while drunk; she considered calling a groupmate; and, much to her own surprise, she thought of calling her mother. Gradually, as group members presented Wilma with their perceptions of her need for mothering, she stopped denying that need. Increasing her contacts with her mother, she began realizing the woman's emotional limitations, both past and present. The process of integrating her baby-self into her self-image had begun. Gradually she became able to deal with her dependency needs instead of avoiding them. She also learned to contact her individual psychotherapist in more appropriate ways when she needed him between sessions. At last she began to freely acknowledge her need for love.

Insight provided by groupmates has been called "benign mirroring" (Pines, 1982), implying, it would seem, that mirroring can at times be antitherapeutic. Members' responses may not always promote change; instead they may reinforce old pathological adaptations. Betty was seen as an extremely valuable group member. Apropos of acting out, we described Betty's history of exhibitionistic behavior. She interrupted group silences, was lively and animated, and presented her personal problems in an entertaining way—all of which the group received with accolades and admiration. Although her exhibitionistic needs and her inability to tolerate silence were perfunctorily acknowledged by Betty and the group, they never became the focus of therapeutic work. Her personal need to avoid anxiety colluded with the group's preference for being entertained, a fact that prevented Betty from taking a more expanded view of herself that might include the sources of her anxiety.

In other instances, mirroring is both available and benign, but patients do not accept it or use it. Instead they respond with rejecting complaints, attributing their lack of progress to the worthless help offered by group therapists and members. These patients become a mirror to others, aggressively showing their perception of the group as not good enough for them. This hostile devaluation of the group's therapeutic efforts induces, in therapists and groupmates alike, a profoundly hopeless sense of therapeutic defeat together with self-accusations and increasingly weakening rescue fantasies. A massive projection of the patient's own hopelessness can be seen to have occurred; these individuals attribute responsibility for the treatment's failure to the therapists and the group instead of acknowledging their personal responsibility.

During the course of a long-term treatment involving many therapeutic modalities, Karen's continual check forging came to

light. When one of the therapists confronted her with this behavior, she violently denied it, accusing the therapist of maligning
her. Other group members joined Karen in her denial and also
in her violent attacks against the therapists. The group members
resonated with Karen's distortion of the therapists, viewing them
as replicas of their abusers. Denial and projection of self-destructiveness prevailed. But when Karen was arrested for her forgeries,
the group atmosphere changed. Group members finally joined
the therapists in mirroring back to Karen the parts of herself that
were self-destructive and unwilling to accept responsibility.
Karen responded to these reflections with pessimism and a sense
of utter hopelessness, as if she were totally unable to do anything
about her behavior. She implied, moreover, that someone
else—boyfriend, parole officer, treaters—should deal with her
problem. Because Karen is sometimes unable to make use of her
groupmates' empathic mirroring, she listens to their perceptions
of her but contemptuously proclaims them useless. In turn, the
group members partly accept these suggestions of their worth-
lessness and failure, and become pessimistic about the group's
helpfulness. Thus Karen's self-destructiveness corrodes the
group's self-image. Her hostility extends beyond herself to the
whole group, which she treats as a bad self-object (i.e., a bad
mother).

Mirroring may sometimes facilitate the integration of the
self, but at other times it is not sufficient. When mirroring does
not lead to therapeutic insights, the missing factor is the proactive
core of the patient's self. Its absence determines the lack of
healthy initiative; facing the choice of going on with life or choosing to die, the patient remains paralyzed, tacitly opting for the
slow equivalent of suicide. Thus some very disturbed patients
cannot use the available mirroring to therapeutic effect; like
Karen, they have sustained such severe damage to the self that
its survival—the will to go on living—may be seriously jeopar-
dized.

Chapter 5

Psychopathology Induced by Defenses After Incest

Psychoanalytic theories of trauma, conflict, and deficit contribute in varying degrees to our understanding of the pathogenesis of the psychiatric symptoms induced by consummated incest. Here we will describe from a psychodynamic viewpoint that relates symptomatology to defense mechanisms, the wide range of psychopathology that derives from incest. Defenses have the curiously dual effect of protecting the individual from mental pain and danger while also producing symptoms; they have both adaptive and maladaptive consequences. Mental pain and danger may originate either in intrapsychic conflict or in environmental trauma. Often there is a combination of both; these cases we label "composite," in contrast to "singular" cases in which psychopathology is derived primarily from trauma. As we have already explored the deficit theory in chapter 4, we will not discuss it here. In what follows we rely on clinical observations of 40 patients we have treated—jointly or separately, in group or individual psychotherapy—as well as on 50 cases about which we were consulted. We were able to obtain limited follow-up on some of these patients after the completion of treatment in various modalities: hypnosis, psychotropic medication, hospitalization, and group, marital, sexual, or individual psychotherapy.

Trauma and Defenses

The study of post-traumatic stress disorder in combat veterans provided a new understanding of symptoms that also affect victims of rape or incest. Incest meets the DSM–III diagnostic criteria for post-traumatic stress disorder, as it involves:

(a) the *existence of a recognizable stressor* that would cause distress in almost anyone; (b) the *reexperiencing of the trauma* with either intrusive recollections of the event, recurrent dreams about it, or sudden feelings and actions experienced as if the traumatic event were reoccurring; (c) *numbing of responsiveness* to or reduced involvement with the external world, beginning after the trauma; (d) some of the following *symptoms*—hyperalertness or exaggerated startle response, sleep disturbances, guilt about surviving, memory impairment or trouble concentrating, avoidance of activities that arouse recollection of the traumatic event, and intensification of symptoms by exposure to events that resemble the traumatic event. [p. 137]

The numbing of responsiveness to the environment, or reduced involvement with it, does protect the individual from the pain experienced *during* the traumatic event, but the *prolongation* of such numbness is an overreaction of the "stimulus barrier" (Freud, 1920) or "modulation of stimulus input" (Horowitz, 1976). Many post-traumatic stress disorder symptoms are the product of this attempt, through "modulation of stimulus input," to help the mental apparatus "not perceive" the environmental assault on the individual.

Incest is a special form of trauma, in that often it is repeated over a span of several years rather than occurring only once or a few times. The secrecy surrounding the breaking of the incest taboo, and the fact that the abuser is a family member who insists on keeping the secret, makes incest trauma especially difficult. Guilt and a sense of betrayal combine to make it almost unbearable. As with every post-traumatic stress disorder, the consequences of the incest trauma go through alternating phases of denial and intrusion. Long periods of forgetting are interrupted by occasional or repeated flashbacks involving certain details of the trauma.

The theory of cognitive processing in the absence of actions help us understand the protracted termination of internalized stress states and the symptomatic responses that persist or start up after the actual termination of the external stress events. A completion tendency is a specific property of cognitive processes. A "need to match" new information with schemata based on older information, and the revision of both until new concordant schemata are achieved, is called a "completion tendency" (Horowitz, 1976). Fistinger (1957) and French (1952) describe similar forms of cognitive processing. Some authors postulate that memory tends to investigate a "next step" in the cognitive processing. Because this process is an intrinsic property of memory, it has been labeled "active memory" (Horowitz, 1976). It may well explain the intrusive stress-event recollections that recur for a long time. The hypothesis of an active memory is compatible with several experimental findings in the fields of perception, attention, and memory. Broadbent (1971) has summarized this research.

Horowitz (1976) notes that "in spite of the conscious experience of intrusiveness, . . . the end result of these repetitions might be adaptation" (p. 102). The cognitive process leads to a revision of automatic information processing and to the invention of new solutions, thus completing the processing of the stressful information. "In psychotherapy of stress-response syndromes, the process of using conscious awareness for change is of central importance" (p. 102). But "consciousness is not the goal, it is . . . a tool for unlearning automatic associations. The goal is to alter the maneuvers by which the stress-related ideas are warded off. Change is accomplished by revisions, learning, and the creation of new solutions" (p. 103). The oscillation between phases of repetition and phases of denial is a form of "dosing." Each repetition leads to a tolerable unit of ideational and affective response.

The theory of cognitive processing gives a detailed description of how "modulation of stimulus input" occurs as to enable the mental apparatus to modulate the ego functions of attention, perception, consciousness, and—above all—memory. The defense mechanisms that operate in the context of active memory are repression, splitting, denial, and projection; each of these attempts to eliminate painful mental contents from the fields of awareness and memory. These mechanisms, which facilitate the cognitive processing of incest trauma, seem to operate in only one way, creating relatively "singular" cases, in contrast to those produced by the "composite" action of the several defense mechanisms mobilized when neurotic conflict prevails and symptoms result as compromise formations. We will discuss these singular cases first and deal later with composite ones.

Defense mechanisms brought into play against the mental pain of incest trauma may alter the ego functions of attention, perception, memory, or consciousness, causing perceptual distortion, amnesia, or dissociative states. We shall review in this connection the pathogenic effects of repression, splitting, denial, identification with the aggressor, introjection, and projection.

Repression

Repression, a defense mechanism that operates unconsciously, denies unacceptable mental contents access to consciousness. These contents are representations, whether ideational, affective, or motor, of instinctual impulses.

Incest mobilizes all the motives that activate repression: guilt, anxiety, shame, and pain. Repression may then act as an anesthesia, providing either a "blackout" of consciousness or a complete amnesia for the distressing facts.

Delayed mastery can gradually occur as the traumatized ego actively works through or elaborates previously repressed memories that appear again and again. One of us once treated a young single woman who during three years of group psychotherapy made significant progress solidifying her previously confused feminine identity. She remembered that her father had bathed and dried her when she was a child, and recalled specific occasions when she had become frightened when he touched her buttocks and genitals. She remembered her father reassuring her that he would not hurt her, saying: "I am your father, I am not going to do you any harm." These memories recurred a number of times and were accompanied by a curiosity to recall more, but also by anxiety and anger at her father.

By the time this patient terminated she had improved considerably. Several years later she contacted the therapist and reported that under hypnosis she had recovered memories of her father's having completed sexual intercourse with her on several occasions when she was thirteen. The extent of her amnesia became surprisingly evident to her when she realized that she had also repressed all recollection of a deformed great-aunt who lived with the family during those years, and who had received at that time considerable attention from the patient.

During group meetings this patient had reported peculiar, hallucination-like experiences at night. The presence of a "monster" in her bedroom was convincingly felt by her. Mainly eyes, this creature limited his activities to peering at her; having no specific shape, it was perceived more as a "presence" than as an image. The patient reacted to these incidents with intense

anxiety, anger, and shame. Her description of the monster was
received by the group with a mixture of support and a concern
for her sanity. The therapist wondered if her altered perception
was an hallucination of the sort described by Ellenson (1985,
1986). These "elementary hallucinatory experiences" were reported in incest victims who repressed their sexual abuse; they
always occurred at night when the patients were alone in bed.
This patient had had her experiences before she had undergone
hypnosis, while she was still repressing specific recollections of
her incest.

On another occasion we consulted on a patient with a similar
mixture of amnesia and vague memories of incest. She recalled
a scene in a corridor when her father had grabbed her from behind
and fondled her breasts. Her mother, surprising them, yelled
"What are you doing?!" and ordered the patient to her room to
wait there for her. The patient recalled running terrified to her
room in anticipation of her mother's scolding. She waited anxiously, but her mother never appeared. Ever after, the patient
fluctuated between doubting the whole thing ever happened and
being convinced that it did. She blamed herself for accusing her
father without just cause, and yet wanted to find out what had
actually occurred. When we recommended hypnosis to explore
her repressed memories, she oscillated between fear of discovering the "awful truth" and anticipation at the prospect of remembering and thus ending the pain of constant doubt. Her fear
of having her mind flooded with unbearable flashbacks needed
to be allayed by reassurances that afterward she would have
control of what was remembered. Frequently she had spontaneous
experiences at night when she felt as if someone were sitting on
the edge of her bed and breathing heavily, like a man sexually
aroused. These flashbacks upset her and made it difficult for her
to go back to sleep. Following our recommendation, she under-
went hypnosis. Instructed that although in a trance she could
select a scene to work on, she chose a situation in which she was

the victim of an attempted sexual assault by a peer, an assault from which she managed to escape. She woke feeling relaxed, in control, and proud of herself. This therapeutic achievement was a turning point in her treatment; for the first time she felt "in charge," no longer at the mercy of painful memories of victimization.

Another woman, who had been sexually molested by her grandfather, exemplifies the repression of feelings, despite clear and detailed memories of the actual molestation. She had no doubt about what had happened between her and "Grandpa." He had kissed her directly on the lips, inserting his tongue in her mouth, and had fondled her breasts. He would pay her in accordance with how well she had satisfied him. He solicited similar sexual favors from other young women in the family. The girls compared experiences and joked about the "dirty old man." The adults in this family encouraged the girls to tolerate this behavior, and denied its seriousness. This combination of tolerance, denial, and humorous reference to Grandpa's activities went on for years.

The patient described her incestuous experiences as if they were very funny, completely unaware of the likely relationship between her current sexual difficulties and her past. She conveyed no sense of anxiety, fear, anger, or guilt. The main concomitant affect was humor. She was obviously denying the seriousness of incest, while repressing the more dysphoric affects involved. She was also identifying herself with the aggressor, as her preferred sexual stimulation was to behave sadistically with her sexual partner. She subjugated him, abused him verbally, and needed to strike him to achieve full orgasm. Unconsciously she was dominating and abusing her partner, just as her grandfather had dominated and abused her.

Regarding the protective function of repression, it may be pertinent to ask what leads these individuals, at a given moment in their lives, to seek the retrieval of incestuous memories? The women described above had recently been faced with painful and

irrefutable evidence of failure in their sexual lives and were compelled to search for possible solutions.

Repression interacting with the repetition compulsion pro-
duces many of the symptoms of post-traumatic stress disorder
and simultaneously offers opportunities for delayed mastery of
the trauma. As in the treatment of any post-traumatic syndrome,
therapists may use these opportunities to promote working
through of the traumatic events, thus imitating the psyche's spontaneous attempts to provide healing through the unlearning of
automatic associations and the search for new solutions.

Splitting

Splitting is a schizoid mechanism described by Melanie
Klein (1946) whereby the incipient ego mentally cuts off unacceptable aspects of the self or of its objects. The cutting off of
parts of the self is comparable to a lizard's automatic response
to a life-threatening situation. When caught by the tail, the lizard
reacts with reflexes that allow the tip of the tail to fall away,
thereby facilitating the animal's flight from danger.

The splitting of objects leads to their being characterized as
either "all bad" persecutors or "all good" idealized objects. By
taking refuge in the relationship with the idealized object, the self
is protected from the threatening persecutors.

Although some of the effects of splitting may superficially
resemble those of repression (i.e., the elimination from awareness
of certain unbearable mental contents), splitting operates much
earlier in life, basically as a protection against aggression's ex-
terminating threats (i.e., paranoid anxiety). Later in life, repression helps the more mature individual deal with fears predominantly
connected with sexual impulses (i.e., castration anxiety).

Splitting of the self becomes pathogenic in victims of incest,
contributing to the development of a false self, such syndromes
as multiple personality, and also to disturbances in integration

between the mental and the bodily selves—sexual dysfunction, hypochondriasis, and anorexia. These symptoms will be described in the present section, except for the last two; these will be examined when we come to discuss composite cases.

Among one hundred patients diagnosed as having multiple personality disorder, estimates of the percentage abused as children ranged between 90 and 97 percent (Putnam, Post, Guroff, et al., 1983). Coons and Milstein (1986), specifying the abuse as sexual, found an incidence of 75 percent in a sample of twenty patients similarly afflicted.

Multiple personality disorder is one of five dissociative disorders listed in DSM-III. Braun and Sachs (1985) note that "a temporary alteration in the awareness of one's identity" characterizes the fluctuations in integrative functions and consciousness, typical of persons with multiple personality disorder. The barrier between the different personalities can be conceptualized as the product of splitting. Instead of sustaining a continuous identity, these individuals may take on a new identity or personality. This alternative personality may be aware of the original or "host" personality, but the host personality usually claims lack of awareness of the other personalities and their actions. Later on, Braun and Sachs point out, "chronic abuse stimulates repeated dissociations which, when chained together by a shared affective state, develop into a personality with a unique identity and behavioral repertoire" (p. 46). Braun (1984) proposes a useful analogy between computers and multiple personality disorders saying that it is almost as if two separate memory systems are created; Memory System 'B', split off from Memory 'A', contains that information which System A was unwilling or could not integrate. This information is often centered around a common theme.

In chapter 4 we mentioned a patient who suffered from multiple personality; whenever she discussed the incest, she became again the little girl who had been violated. She spoke in the partial sentences typical of baby talk and was unable to take care of herself in basic ways. At other times she was completely unaware of having behaved like a little girl, and was unable to recall what had occurred while the childlike state prevailed.

The development of a false self, and the splitting off of the inchoate true self, can occur as a complication of incest. One patient described herself as "not knowing which part of herself was real" because she grew up having constantly to please others. For long periods during which her mother was absent from the home the patient was left in the care of male family members, a number of whom engaged in sex with her. Her mother's absence left the patient hungry for emotional nurturance. In a family consisting of several siblings, she developed a capacity to be charming and appealing, but in a childlike manner fraught with sexual overtones. Her coquettish demeanor was taken to be sexual, and she thereby obtained her portion of care within the family's competitive atmosphere. Her current appeals for attention, ongoing attempts to feed her emotional starvation, continue to be mixed with coquettish expressions of her femininity. Her false self strives to please others, both interpersonally and sexually, while her true self remains hidden and confused because of lack of definition. Her facial expression reflects her confusion: she perpetually squints, as if trying to emerge from a mental fog. Her real self is connected to a pervasive sense of shame, as if her need for attention, which has contributed to her sexual involvement with several male relatives, made her unacceptable.

Sexual dysfunction is a relatively frequent consequence of incest. One patient, for instance, is anorgastic and feels ashamed that she is not "a complete woman"; she likes sex only because she has felt nurtured by sexual contacts, first with her father and now with other men. Another patient, though able to experience multiple orgasm, must first overcome considerable initial anxiety with each sexual contact. Furthermore, the conditions under which sex is pleasurable for her are limited: she cannot have sex in the dark, and she needs always to be in control. She worries that her capacity for multiple orgasm is an indication that she is "loose"; she feels ashamed of what she considers her body's overreaction. The circumstances of her incestuous experiences conditioned these limitations: her brother had abused her during the night, appearing abruptly in her bed and covering her mouth to muffle her protests while they had intercourse.

The splitting of objects into "persecutors" and "idealized" objects protects the self from persecutory anxiety: the ideal object is a refuge. One patient, who was sexually abused by her brothers, sees ministers as ideal men, while she views physicians as villains. Physicians, however, initially appear to her as if they find her attractive; she has even entertained erotic fantasies about some, before turning them into sadistic enemies.

Another woman, sexually abused by her father, suffered from psychosis; she had auditory hallucinations. These voices criticized and blamed her for her sexual behavior with her father, whom she idealized; she declared herself in love with him and wished to continue their sexual liaison. Her father shared this wish, making sex between them acceptable and reinforcing his role as an apparent good object who protected her from criticism. Thus the patient had to project her superego reproaches outside of her, to externalize them as voices.

Denial

Denial, a primitive defense mechanism that forms the core of manic reactions, defends against depressive anxieties experienced as guilt, sadness, and loss. Denial makes life look "rosy" by eliminating acknowledgment of such painful aspects of psychic reality as ambivalence toward lost objects and dependency on them. By allowing the individual to focus on the brighter side of life, denial often promotes health. If used excessively, however, it creates distortions of reality and a lack of psychological-mindedness. The value of objects is not recognized and they may be treated contemptuously, in a controlling manner yielding self-aggrandizement and a sense of triumph. The presence of psychic pain is ignored and no efforts are made to relieve it. The anesthetizing action of alcohol, stimulants, and sedatives may enhance denial, as may orgiastic activities such as promiscuity, overeating, partying, overspending, and reckless driving. The latter are varieties of acting out, a topic explored in greater depth in chapter 3.

Identification with the Aggressor

Identification with the aggressor is a complex defense first described by Anna Freud (1936). Victims use this mechanism to cope with humiliation, pain, and helplessness; no longer passive, they achieve delayed mastery by doing to others what had previously been done to them. Identification with the aggressor explains the frequent shift from victim to abuser among persons with a history of incest; it also illuminates the intergenerational transmission of incestuous behavior.

We described Wilma's case in chapter 3. Finding herself in love with a younger man, she initially was unaware that her behavior replicated certain aspects of her father's conduct with her. However, she became severely depressed and entertained ideas of suicide. These represented an unconscious attempt to rid herself of the "abuser within," the one who was tempted to seduce a young man. The therapists' interpretation of the meaning of her unconscious identification with the aggressor gradually relieved her guilt and heightened her awareness of the abusive connotations of the relationship.

Identification with the aggressor reverses the roles of victim and abuser, creating a complex web of interaction between introjection and projection. Confused identity may be transitorily experienced, obscuring the individual's status as victim or abuser.

Introjection does not necessarily result in identification. It is possible to introject an object without incorporating it into the self. The mental presence of the internalized but unassimilated object is experienced instead as separate or different from the self. But when the self incorporates and assimilates the internalized object, the self becomes its replica and identification has occurred. When Wilma caught herself wishing to treat her young man as her father had treated her, she started hating herself—"The shadow of the object fell upon the ego" (Freud, 1917, p. 249). But she could also project herself onto her young man, attributing to him feelings she had experienced herself when seduced by her father. For example, she believed that her boyfriend felt flattered, yet scared, at having been chosen, and that he enjoyed being admired and needed as a caretaker while resenting being treated as a possession.

Conflict and Defenses

The concept of conflict refers to the dynamic struggles between drives attempting to be discharged or gratified, and the defenses opposing such discharge because of anxiety, guilt, or shame. Such struggles occur in the realm of internal psychic reality or unconscious fantasy.

Certain conflicts are landmarks in the emotional development of human beings. These include the Oedipus complex, the depressive position, and struggles against envy and the psychotic part of the personality. Freud discovered the child in the adult; Melanie Klein wrote about the infant in all of us; and Bion explored the psychotic part of the human mind, in groups and otherwise.

The oedipal conflict centers around the unconscious wish to consummate incest with the parent of the opposite sex, while eliminating the parent of the same sex. It therefore places the individual in a triangular situation, feeling anxious about possible punishment for sexual wishes (castration anxiety), jealous over being put off by the loved object, enraged vis-à-vis the parent of the same sex, and guilty. This guilt may induce self-mutilation. Two of our patients had this symptom.

Most defense mechanisms described by Anna Freud (1936) are active against this conflict, which occurs when incipient sexual interests appear in a relatively advanced stage of development. Repression, negation, reaction-formation, isolation, undoing, projection, introjection, turning against the self, and transformation into the opposite may all be utilized in the struggle against oedipal conflicts.

Melanie Klein (1935, 1940) described the depressive position. The focus of this conflict is guilt over devouring a loved object. The main developmental task in the depressive position is to integrate the mother as a part-object—the feeding breast—with the mother as a whole object, a sexual being linked to the father. Her "good" and "bad" features are put together with love and hate for her. Just as splitting characterizes the schizo-paranoid position, so integration forms the core of the depressive position. Weaning starts incipient movements to separate from the mother, thus losing her and promoting a wish to repair the fantasied damage to her, leading in turn to an internalized good object within the individual's mind. Freud's "Mourning and Melancholia" (1917) and Melanie Klein's studies of mourning and manic-depressive states (1935, 1940) significantly contributed to our understanding of the defense mechanisms against depressive conflict, mainly introjection of the lost object and subsequent identification with it. The successful working through of the depressive position facilitates the child's separation from its mother. Klein contributed to systematizing the "manic defenses" against guilt, loss, sadness, and frustrated dependency. These defenses are omnipotent denial and a style of dealing with objects whereby the subject feels triumphant over the object, who is experienced as controlled and devalued.

Klein pursued the study of early states of emotional development, which she first grouped and labeled as "the phase of maximum sadism" (1932) and later as the "schizo-paranoid position" (1946). She described splitting and projection as prevailing defenses during that stage. She also studied the struggles of the human infant against envy (1957): the conflict between the infant's own greedy emptiness and the maternal breast's fullness and richness—an elementary, primordial version of the conflict between the "haves" and the "have nots." Klein described the early defenses against envy: omnipotence, denial, splitting, confusion (as a specific way of counteracting persecutory anxieties), devaluation of the self, and provocation of another's envy.

Grinberg (1985) delineated several psychopathological expressions of the "psychotic part of the personality," expressions described by Bion as "extreme defenses": acting out, negative therapeutic reaction, "reversed perspective," "impasse," and somatization. All these defenses are expressions of the psychotic part of the mind. Grinberg elaborates Bion's description of the psychotic part of the personality, reflecting on the ways it expresses itself in the psychoanalytic situation. (Chapter 3 presents examples of somatization and splitting of the object and of the self; chapter 4 concludes with a discussion of the negative therapeutic reaction.)

Bion's notion of "reversed perspective" (1966) refers to the different perceptions, in the classical gestalt experiment on visual perception, whereby it is possible to see the same figure in two entirely different ways depending on perspective (i.e., either as a vase or as two profiles facing each other). A manifest agreement between patient and analyst may coexist with a latent and radical disagreement according to which the patient "sees" everything going on in the psychoanalytic situation in a perspective completely different from that of the analyst. Patients of this sort do not care about understanding their problems but instead strive to demonstrate a greater capacity to understand themselves than is demonstrated by their analysts. This kind of parallel and hidden "contract," silent and sly, is sometimes difficult to detect (Grinberg, 1985). The "reversed perspective" makes patients behave as if they were their own analysts. There are important parallels between Bion's "reversed perspective" of patients in analysis and the "parentified" behavior of incest victims: in incestuous families children are pushed into acting as parents to their own parents and also into doing their own parenting.

Effects of Combined Defenses: Composite Cases

In contrast to simpler cases in which it is possible to trace the effects of a single defense against trauma affecting the functions of memory, perception, attention, or consciousness, more complicated cases result from the combined action of multiple defense mechanisms against trauma and conflicts. We will describe briefly here a few such composite cases. A more detailed description of two cases will follow.

Splitting may produce a mind/body cleavage of the self whereby unbearable mental contents are eliminated from awareness and stress is referred to preoccupations with the body. Incest may foster this split because most incestuous experiences have a central physical component, with the body often responding to sexual stimulation; sometimes specifically orgastic pleasure happens as a physiological answer to stimulation beyond the individual's mental control. This natural cleavage may be further enhanced by a need to get rid of the painful, confusing, and dysphoric emotional responses elicited by incest. Out-of-body reactions whereby the mind "leaves the body" and looks at it "from a distance" have frequently been reported by incest victims. Sometimes they may trigger these reactions simply by concentrating their attention on the wallpaper in the room or on distant fantasized scenes; at other times these reactions occur as an expression of hate for the body's betrayal into pleasurable responsivity (see chapter 3).

Hypochondriacal anxiety can be explained as a product of the mind/body cleavage, operating so that the basic fear of "losing one's mind" is denied by way of concern with various bodily malfunctions. A widespread paranoid anxiety, fear of loss of the self, is thus restricted to concerns with losing a single organ or bodily function. The bodily part that is the core of such hypochondriacal anxiety is connected—in the patient's mind—with some persecutor with whom the patient has become partially identified. Hypochondriasis can be described as a kind of persecutory, quasi-delusional syndrome whereby the persecution occurs within the self, the persecutory attack being launched from within the body.

Another example of a mind/body cleavage in which all preoccupations are defensively centered on the body is anorexia nervosa. This condition is, according to Rizzuto, Peterson, and Reed (1981), an altered relationship between the bodily sense of self and the psychic self. . . . Anorectics feel that their parents can acknowledge only their physical presence and discount their "yearning for recognition of their psychic self". In chapter 3 we discussed a patient who looks like a model but sees herself as fat; her incestuous abuser had told her she was fat and promised she would lose weight from intercourse with him because of profuse perspiration. The focus of this patient's distress is her body. She denies any emotional problems, except to say that her partner unreasonably demands sex. Although she becomes depressed after spending time with him, she sees no connection between the two circumstances and cannot grasp the incongruity of spending leisure time with a man she professes to hate so intensely. For her, the problem resides in her body and her partner. She lacks sexual desire, yet she does not see her sexual difficulties as a dysfunction that needs to be corrected. In the treatment she goes through the motions but evidencing a certain contentment with her current situation.

We will now describe in detail two composite cases.

Betty[1]

Betty has been in psychiatric treatment throughout her life, beginning at age six, when she suffered from enuresis, and continuing until age fifty-two, when we saw her in consultation for problems emanating from her experience of incest.

Betty's mother sought help in correcting her daughter's bed wetting, which began shortly after the birth of a half-sister. Her father preferred the younger daughter. Intensely jealous of this new sister, Betty felt unwanted. However, she explicitly denied any rivalry, instead claiming that the baby was her favorite sibling.

There was no report then of incest, though Betty would later tell treaters that her brother had been sexually abusing her since she was six. Instead she alluded to her discomfort with the lack of boundaries in the family home, explicitly expressing her wish for a private bathroom with a door. She appeared preoccupied with neatness and orderliness, the first clinical observation of her obsessive traits. But though the incest was occurring, she did not mention it to her first psychiatrist. Probably she was scared; obviously she was denying the experience. And even at this young age she displayed an ability to charm like a witty actress, thus hiding her low self-esteem.

Betty's next contact with psychiatric services occurred during her mid-twenties, after she had suffered a series of "panic attacks." Intense panic led her to withdraw from people and stay at home. Later her condition evolved into agoraphobia.

Her third psychiatric consultation was sought because of inhibited sexual desire. By then she had entered a stable common-law marriage. During their early years together, the couple's sexual life was very gratifying. They were uninhibited and used

---

[1]Since the case of Betty is used as an illustration throughout the book, we are not repeating previously discussed material about her. For a complete overview of this case we suggest reading vignettes about her in chapters, 2, 3, and 4.

shared sexual fantasies to stimulate themselves. Group sex was a favorite fantasy, and involved wishes to observe the other having sexual intercourse with a third party. These fantasies were realized when they engaged in group sex with Betty's best girlfriend. During the second experience of group sex, however, the patient suffered a dissociative episode in which she experienced herself as outside her own body and observing from a distance. She refused intercourse, the group sex ceased, and her relationship with her girlfriend was broken off. At the time of the third consultation, Betty had not regained her sexual desire. She became depressed and her phobia worsened: whenever her husband left home, she panicked. This condition was treated with behavioral modification techniques, which increased her mobility somewhat but did not correct her inhibited sexual desire.

Several years later she relapsed, her phobias returned, and she again sought treatment. The relapse was precipitated by a change of residence and an inability to stay in her new home alone. In this fourth psychiatric consultation Betty disclosed her history of incest for the first time. Her brother—six years her senior—had molested her from the age of three until she became seriously ill in early adolescence. She remembered his performing oral sex on her and fondling her, as well as asking her to perform oral sex with him. When she told her mother, she was reprimanded for the "terrible thing" she was doing. Betty did not mention it again. Diagnosed in this fourth consultation as having a histrionic personality disorder, she began concurrent individual and group psychotherapy, later supplemented with sex therapy.

The patient was the third child in a family of four children, including two older brothers and a younger sister. The patient's relationship with her father was difficult. The family atmosphere was chaotic, characterized by violent fights, lack of boundaries, and extreme poverty. Betty's mother died suddenly when the patient was a young adult.

The patient was born with a congenital heart defect. This

condition led her to believe that she would die young and also induced fears in her husband that sex with her might cause her death. In Betty's mind, sex, fatal illness, and panic were intertwined.

At the time Betty began treatment with us, she was in midlife but looked younger and dressed like a college student. She is blonde, intense, articulate, and charming. She is also intelligent in a practical way, knowing how to deal with people, although she is socially unsophisticated. She tends to manipulate those who interact with her, and constantly attempts to control the conversation. She appeared very "treatment-wise." Sometimes she is able to exercise her control more subtly, displaying friendliness and warmth mixed with humor and vivaciousness. She presents herself as an entertainer in search of an audience. She sees herself as a nonconformist who is superficially compliant. With her charm, she succeeds in getting her own way, usually without irritating others.

She is quite anxious, tending toward a high level of activity, often with a counterphobic quality reinforced by hypomanic displays that help fight a depressive proclivity. She seldom cries, but may become intensely and dramatically angry and jealous. She tends to feel worthless, with a "rotten body" that will let her down and cause her to die young. She sees herself as a member of the lower classes, feeling like an impostor when she socializes with middle-class people. She is pleased with her body's capacity for multiple orgasm but fears she will become a "loose woman." She also experiences herself as a victim of incest, poverty, and poor health. However, she is also a survivor who compensates for all her self-doubts by struggling against adversity, sometimes to the extent of trying to be a "Superwoman." Even during her darkest times, she manages to feel hopeful; she has rarely given up. She is adaptable and practical, especially when managing money. She harbors a fear that once again she might become poor; thus money and possessions are important to her. She exhibits no evidence of memory difficulties, hallucinations, or delusional beliefs.

Betty was eager to begin individual and group psychotherapy focused on the emotional scars of incest. She expressed relief at finding a group of peers who shared similar incestuous experiences, and valued her ties with them from the start.

After approximately a year of group psychotherapy, during a session at which the female therapist was absent, Betty distorted an intervention by the male therapist regarding her unconscious identification with the aggressor. She felt extremely abused by him. In this she was supported by several group members who perceived the episode as an "emotional rape," which in their eyes justified her violent demand for an apology. (This incident is described in detail in chapter 1).

Shortly afterward, Betty had a relapse of her heart condition which required hospitalization. Group members frequently visited her there, and the cotherapists talked with her by phone. Betty felt reassured that she was accepted and appreciated by peers and treaters alike. When she returned to the group, she was able to resume psychotherapeutic work with both therapists. Appreciative of the therapists' interest in her physical health, she began to speak of her gratitude toward her abusive brother for teaching her the streetwise tricks of survival. For the first time she was able to cry in the group.

A productive period of treatment ensued. Betty's agoraphobia decreased, allowing her to move more freely and to travel. She developed a capacity to anticipate her panic attacks and to counteract them with insight. Her relationship with her husband improved. Betty was also able to review her problems with her drug-dependent daughter, in the context of discussing a young group member's problems.

Unconscious jealousy became prominent when a new member entered the group, but Betty steadfastly denied any rivalrous feelings. However, during this new member's first group session,

Betty hinted guiltily that she might have contributed to the sexual abuse of her younger sister: she had gone along with her brothers idea of including the sister in group sex. Betty was never able to work through her severe jealousy conflicts in the group. Shortly after the arrival of this new patient she decided to leave the group, rationalizing her decision.

Betty needed to defend herself against major conflicts, both oedipal and depressive, as well as against envy and the psychotic layers of her mind. The oedipal conflict had led her to feel intense rivalry with anyone who took her mother away from her, be it father or younger sister. She also experienced an inverted oedipal conflict. Not having worked through the depressing loss of her mother as exclusively hers, she instead hypomanically denied both the loss and any need for her mother. She was also envious of her mother's power and had already become a "parentified" child. "Extreme defenses," typical of the functioning of the psychotic part of the mind, had already been called into action by Betty's unconscious. During her first psychiatric consultation she denied her jealousy of her newborn sister; already she was resorting to somatization (the enuresis), in an attempt to focus her problems in her body rather than in her mind. She also denied the incestuous experience, even as she used elaborate hypomanic defenses and exhibitionistic behaviors to charm the psychiatric examiner.

Betty was jealous mainly of her mother's preference for the men in their family. The envy of men she unconsciously experienced gave rise to exhibitionistic behavior as a defense against castration anxiety. Exhibitionism and voyeurism were central to her sexual fantasies and preferences. Possibly she identified with her aggressive brother by assuming the role of abuser with her younger sister. Later on, she developed a similarly sadistic style in dealing with significant others, including her therapists. But she also turned her sadism against herself, developing a masochistic style of self-punishment.

Betty split her self into a false self, with which she tried to please and placate everybody, and a real self, which anxiously needed to go underground. She hated her body for threatening her with early death, while she glamorized her mind and intellect. She also split her objects (i.e., her father against her mother, one treater against another). Her repression of the traumatic memories of incest occasionally failed, so that at times she experienced flashbacks. That she waged these defensive struggles against trauma reminds us that the distinction between defenses against conflicts and defenses protecting from trauma is merely conventional.

Alice

Alice, young, single, and white, was referred for psychiatric consultation by a neurologist because, though she was unable to walk and was anesthesic from the waist down, the neurological examination had revealed no organic basis for these symptoms. What seemed, then, to be conversion symptoms appeared after she had become engaged to her longstanding boyfriend.

Following her decision to marry, Alice recalled having been sexually abused during latency by several family members. The first incident she remembered was that she had been raped by two brothers—two and four years older than she—while their male friends held her down. However, the details of this incident were then vague in her memory.

Alice's psychiatrist realized her intense aversion to sexuality and told her initially that marriage was not an option for her at this time. Her neurological symptoms then subsided, but she became less motivated for psychotherapy.

Alice appeared very anxious; wide-eyed, she looked about her with darting, furtive glances, as if anticipating some terrifying event at any moment. She was reluctant to explore her thoughts and fantasies, but instead expected the therapist to provide her immediate answers and relief. She provided no information spontaneously, communicating her extreme discomfort only nonverbally, by sitting tensely on the edge of her chair. She almost begged the examiner to ask questions but when queried would answer in monosyllables. Ashamed of her secrets, she was unable to use the appropriate terms to describe the incest, resorting instead to vague, oblique references. She held herself responsible for everything that had happened. Frequently she placed herself in dangerous situations with little regard for her own welfare or safety. She was accident-prone. Despite her financial limitations, she insisted on being charged the standard therapy fee, as paying less would have been demeaning. Openly distrustful, she asked the examiner what would be recorded in the notes. Her view of others was extremely fearful and alienating. She saw some people, especially those closest to her, as potential attackers whose reasons she could not understand. She refused to wear skirts because she remembered she had been wearing a dress when she was raped by her brothers. She also expected to be criticized by others if they should learn what she was really like; thus she protected herself by being friendly, compliant, and helpful.

She denied hallucinations and changes in her body image, but acknowledged periods of depersonalization, memory lacunae, and fugue states. For example, on one occasion, unable to account for five hours, she found herself to her surprise in the airport of a strange city. She had no notable delusions, and her intelligence was normal.

The patient's family background was chaotic. The patient's father physically abused the mother and verbally abused the whole family. When Alice was five her father was absent for a year; during this time the patient was first raped by her brothers. Her father was seriously ill for several years and died when Alice was thirteen. In the intervening years she was sexually abused by her brothers on several occasions. Because Alice's father changed jobs frequently, the family made numerous moves. Alice has two older sisters and two older brothers. Her mother was a hard-working, religious woman who seemed to derive a feeling of virtue from her suffering. When Alice would voice dissatisfaction with her, her mother would cry profusely, making Alice feel guilty.

The patient's treatment spanned several years, beginning with individual psychotherapy and including several psychiatric hospitalizations and group psychotherapy.

In the beginning Alice struggled to discuss her incestuous secrets in the face of considerable reluctance. Gradually she progressed from referring to her past as full of vague secrets to referring to the abuse as "rapes" and finally as "incest." She painfully forced herself to talk about these memories, despite the increasing severity of her frequent headaches and an incident in which she fainted after a disagreement with one of her brothers. She somatized mainly through headaches. In desperation, Alice began calling her individual psychotherapist between sessions, but frequently was unable to communicate anything but distress over her headaches. Finally, during one phone call, she was unable to remember the number of pills, which had been prescribed for her headaches, that she had just taken. Alice was terrified of her growing dependency on her therapist, fearing that she would be abused again in this relationship. When the therapist suggested that Alice had the power to decide whether to stay in therapy, she chose to remain, saying that it was time for her to work on important issues such as whether she should marry.

The treatment proceeded smoothly for the first year. As Alice's conflicts over separation intensified, apropos the upcoming summer interruption of treatment by the therapist's vacation, several important events occurred. The patient was dismayed to learn from her mother that a woman with the same name as Alice had been charged with drunken driving. Although Alice disclaimed any knowledge of this situation, the police contacted her with a warrant for her arrest. Shortly thereafter she flunked a polygraph examination in which she denied drug use and stealing. She jokingly commented on how different her namesake was from herself, who was religious and well above reproach. Most likely, however, Alice had experienced dissociative states of consciousness during which she behaved in ways otherwise unacceptable to her. Flashbacks of her sexual abuse began to occur; concomitantly, previously forgotten memories surfaced, some of which concerned her brothers forcing her to participate in the abuse of another woman. She had thoughts of killing herself. On one occasion she called her psychotherapist but became mute after saying hello. Concerned for Alice's safety, the therapist went to her home, where she found the patient painfully reliving the rape, writhing in her bed in an altered state of consciousness. Hospitalization was again indicated, but Alice left after a few hours, convinced the male hospital treaters would harm her. As the therapist's vacation drew closer, Alice's condition worsened, but she refused to return to the hospital and took a trip instead. She thus responded to the therapist's absence by acting out her conflicts. After the summer interruption Alice had to be rehospitalized; this time, however, she stayed the recommended length of time.

For several months Alice explored her sadomasochistic style of interacting within close relationships. During this time she abruptly decided to get married, thus counterphobically throwing herself into the situation she feared most—sexual contact with a man. She reported that she vomited each time after intercourse. Still, her self-respect as a woman was tied to being able to perform sexually. She also decided to study psychology, "just like" the therapist. Shortly after Alice's wedding, her therapist announced another upcoming absence. The patient reported having intercourse with difficulty, but did not talk with her husband about this. Her headaches worsened and she became severely depressed and anxious, entertaining thoughts of suicide. She quit her job. Finally she disclosed that she was forcing herself to have sex two or three times a day, vomiting and passing out afterward. Just before the therapist's absence she had to be hospitalized; but again she left the hospital prematurely, only to be rehospitalized when the therapy resumed. Because of the intensity of Alice's transference to her individual therapist, group and marital treatments were indicated.

Alice regularly attended group psychotherapy twice a week for two years. The only group member with a history of incest, she was ambivalent about participating in the group, withdrawing frequently into angry silence. However, after a year she developed a working alliance in the group: she shared the stories of her early abuse, afterward becoming less inhibited and more trusting. Most of the second year she worked through her conflicts about separation. During the last three months, during which time she was the only female group member, she transferred onto two male group members her long-standing feelings of displeasure toward her brothers.

At the time of her discharge, Alice no longer used confusion as a defense, was more tolerant of her affects, and was better integrated. However, Alice later found it necessary to resume individual treatment and obtained help in another part of the country.

Alice suffered both from the consequences of trauma and from conflicts. She experienced intrusive recollections of the sexual abuse and was flooded with feelings and actions, as if the trauma were reoccurring. She was hyperalert, suffered memory impairment, struggled counterphobically against her spontaneous tendency to avoid sexual activities, and often became more symptomatic after intercourse. All these behaviors are the pathogenic effects of defenses against trauma. Alice's ego functions of memory, consciousness, and identity fluctuated following the "modulation of input" of the traumatic stimuli. She used repression, splitting, and denial extensively.

Alice also struggled with conflicts related to the crucial developmental milestones. She used repression against her sexual anxieties, occasionally identifying herself with the aggressor by regressing to a sadomasochistic style of relating and by developing, as a reaction-formation, an exaggerated interest in sexual activities.

Her crucial conflicts concerned separation. Her intense transferential attachment led to a worsening of symptoms after each therapeutic interrupton. Her thoughts of suicide combined with a need to control the therapist, which later led to her identification with the treater as a psychologist. Group psychotherapy was indicated to diminish the psychotic component in her transference responses.

Alice used splitting both of self and objects; dissociative states and fugues occurred often. She also used "extreme defenses": acting out, various somatizations, and the creation of serious therapeutic impasses.

Like Betty, Alice has an extensive, complex psychopathology associated with the pathogenic effects of defenses against incest trauma and serious conflicts. Both experienced struggles over separation, compounded by intense envy and frequent lapses into a psychotic mode of functioning, with concomitant extreme defenses. Each woman has already spent several years in various treatments. Although both have made considerable progress, in each the struggle of the self to survive continues; both acknowledge that they may need psychiatric help episodically, for many years, so that they may continue to grow.

Discussion

Two different psychoanalytic theories about the etiology of neurosis seem diametrically opposed: one points the finger at trauma, the other at conflict. Initially Freud (Breuer and Freud, 1893–1895) believed in the "seduction theory," according to which sexual trauma would explain neurotic symptoms. When he discovered that psychic reality, or fantasy, could prevail over external reality, he formulated the conflict theory and apparently dropped his earlier seduction theory. However, trauma and conflict phenomena are complementary; preexisting conflicts may ascribe a traumatic meaning, sometimes unconscious or symbolic, even to relatively innocuous external stimuli. What is therefore traumatic for one individual is—within a certain range of stimuli—contingent upon this person's preexistent internal conflicts. Well-balanced individuals may tolerate stimuli that might be stressors for the majority of human beings. On the other hand, recognizable stressors may cause distress in almost anyone, frequently generating additional neurotic conflicts.

The contemporary understanding of post-traumatic stress disorder clarifies how the modulation of stimulus input operates by narrowing the span of attention, even to the point of suppressing some stimuli. Memory can be modulated unconsciously, outside the individual's awareness, resulting in a selective amnesia. Clinicians say that these forgotten memories have undergone repression. The difference between these two mechanisms is that in suppression the victim chooses to focus attention away from the actual trauma, while in repression the person passively experiences a lack of control in retrieving painful remembrances.

The incest trauma complicates normal developmental conflicts so that their resolution becomes considerably more difficult. Trauma and conflict are intertwined in the mind of the incest victim. Reworking nonadaptive resolutions of conflict often requires multiple and protracted treatments—individual, group, marital, and sex therapies, as well as hypnosis, psychotropic medication, and occasional psychiatric hospitalization.

Once it has been established that sexual abuse has occurred, it is tempting for patients and clinicians alike to define the goal of therapy as a quest for truth. After many years of repression, however, a sudden onslaught of painful memories can overwhelm the adult incest victim, with serious negative consequences. Furthermore, "knowing the truth" is often distorted to mean discovering who is to be blamed, with an implicit hope that clarifying the issue will itself eliminate the pain of incest trauma and its psychopathological consequences. If the truth is confirmed, disappointment results when the implicit promise of release and cure is not fulfilled. Clinician and patient are left to struggle with serious psychopathology; the incest trauma continues to work its manifold effects in the patient's mind. Moreover, establishing the objective reality that somebody else was "at fault" externalizes the focus of therapy and leaves the patient's inner conflicts unattended.

The therapist's strategy in dealing with stress response syndromes is instead to bring the traumatic experiences to awareness, as "a tool for unlearning automatic associations" (Horowitz, 1976, p. 103) and for creating new solutions to old conflicts. For example, a major therapeutic task may be to break the connections between sex on the one hand and pain, shame, and guilt on the other. Change is accomplished only gradually, as repeated revisions of the trauma make possible further unlearning of the initial automatic associations to the trauma, and as new solutions of conflicts are tried.

The protracted nature of overcoming the incest trauma and related conflicts has not been generally acknowledged. The major goal of many time-limited treatments is to provide opportunities for catharsis of intense repressed feelings. Rage at the offender, resentment against the mother's abandonment, and an outpouring of the sense of guilt, isolation, and shame are powerful affects that often have been insufficiently expressed. But the abreaction of these feelings should not be confused with finding *practical solutions* to the many problems facing the patient (e.g., the adult victim's confrontation and current relations with the offender; the involvement of other members of the family of origin; and the desire to take revenge through recourse to the law). All these matters require a long period of time and are tremendously variable from person to person. This need for individually tailored treatment plans runs afoul of standardized programs that encourage routine catharsis, followed by identical strategies for all victims vis-à-vis these practical problems. The cathartic goal is useful, but only as a first stage in the long struggle to overcome the consequences of incest.

The cost in time, energy, money, and suffering can be considerable, a fact that puts pressure on treaters to find simple, inexpensive answers to this extremely complex problem. In a very real sense, coping with the aftermath of incest is a lifelong and inescapable challenge, despite the most determined efforts to evade it.

References

Anzieu, D. (1984), *The Group and the Unconscious*, trans. B. Kiborne. London: Routledge & Kegan Paul.

Bacal, H.A. (1983), Object relations in the group from the perspective of self psychology. Presented at the A.G.P.A. Annual Conference, Toronto, February.

Bauman, S. (1981), Physical aspects of the self: A review of some aspects of body image development in childhood. *Psychiat. Clin. N. Amer.*, 4:455–470.

Bion, W.R. (1961), *Experiences in Groups*. London: Tavistock.

——— (1966), *Elements of Psycho-Analysis*. In: *Seven Servants, Part II*. New York: Aronson, 1977, pp. 1–110.

Blake-White, J., & Kline, C. (1985), Treating the dissociative process in adult victims of childhood incest. *Social Casework: J. Contemp. Soc. Work*, 66:394–402.

Bloch, G.R., & Bloch, N.H. (1976), Analytic group psychotherapy of post-traumatic psychoses. *Internat. J. Group Psychother.*, 26:49–57.

Boatman, B., Borkan, E.L., & Schetky, D.H. (1981), Treatment of child victims of incest. *Amer. J. Fam. Ther.*, 9:43–51.

Borriello, J.F., (1973), Patients with acting out character disorders. *Amer. J. Psychother.*, 27:4–14.

——— (1979), Group psychotherapy with acting out patients: Specific problems and techniques. *Amer. J. Psychother.*, 33:521–530.

Braun, B.G. (1984), Towards a theory of multiple personality and other dissociative phenomena. *Psychiat. Clin. N. Amer.*, 7:171–193.

——— Sachs, R.G. (1985), The development of multiple personality disorders: Predisposing, precipitating, and perpetuating factors. In: *Childhood An-*

109

tecedents of Multiple Personality, ed. R. Kluft. Washington, DC: American Psychiatric Press, pp. 38–64.

Breuer, J., & Freud, S. (1893–1895), The psychotherapy of hysteria. *Standard Edition*, 2:255–305. London: Hogarth Press, 1953.

Broadbent, D.E. (1971), *Decision and Stress*. London: Academic Press.

Ciba Foundation (1984), *Child Sexual Abuse Within the Family*, ed. R. Porter. New York: Tavistock.

Cole, C.L. (1985), A group design for adult female survivors of childhood incest. *Women & Therapy*, 4:71–82.

Coons, P.M., & Milstein, V. (1986), Psychosexual disturbances in multiple personality: Characteristics, etiology, and treatment. *J. Clin. Psychiat.*, 47:3.

Corwin, D. (1983), Family treatment of father-daughter incest. In: *Therapeutic Intervention in Father-Daughter Incest* (American Psychiatric Audio Review: Symposium of the 1982 American Psychiatric Association Annual Meeting). Washington, DC: American Psychiatric Press.

Deighton, J., & McPeek, P. (1985), Group treatment: Adult victims of childhood sexual abuse. *Social Casework: J. Contemp. Soc. Work*, 66:403–410.

Ellenson, G.S. (1985), Detecting a history of incest: A predictive syndrome. *Social Casework: J. Contemp. Soc. Work*, 66:525–532.

——— (1986), Disturbances of perception in adult female incest survivors. *Social Casework: J. Contemp. Soc. Work*, 67(3):149–159.

Ezriel, H. (1950), A psychoanalytic approach to group treatment. *Brit. J. Med. Psychol.*, 23:59–74.

——— (1952), Notes on psychoanalytic group psychotherapy: II. Interpretation and research. *Psychiatry*, 15:119–126.

Fairbairn, W.R.D. (1940), Schizoid factors in the personality. In: *An Object-Relations Theory of the Personality*. New York: Basic Books, 1954, p. 5.

——— (1952), *Psychoanalytic Studies of the Personality*. London: Tavistock.

Fistinger, L. (1957), *A Theory of Cognitive Dissonance*. New York: Row, Peterson.

Fowler, C., Burns, S., & Roehl, J.E. (1983), Counseling the incest offender. *Internat. J. Fam. Ther.*, 5:92–97.

French, T. (1952), *The Integration of Behavior: Vol. 1. Basic Postulates*. Chicago: University of Chicago Press.

Freud, A. (1936), *The Ego and the Mechanisms of Defence*. London: Hogarth Press.

——— (1968), Acting out. *Internat. J. Psycho-Anal.*, 49:165–170.

Freud, S. (1905), Fragment of an analysis of a case of hysteria. *Standard Edition*, 7:7–122. London: Hogarth Press, 1953.

——— (1912), The dynamics of transference. *Standard Edition*, 12:99–108. London: Hogarth Press, 1958.

——— (1914a), On narcissism: An introduction. *Standard Edition*, 14:73–102. London: Hogarth Press, 1957.

——— (1914b), Remembering, repeating and working-through. *Standard Edition*, 12:147–156. London: Hogarth Press, 1958.

——— (1917), Mourning and melancholia. *Standard Edition*, 14:243–258. London: Hogarth Press, 1957.

——— (1920), Beyond the pleasure principle. *Standard Edition*, 18:7–64. London: Hogarth Press, 1955.

——— (1931), Female sexuality. *Standard Edition*, 21:225–243. London: Hogarth Press, 1961.

Ganzarain, R. (1983), Working through in analytic group psychotherapy. *Internat. J. Group Psychother.*, 33:281–296.

Garcia Marquez, G. (1985), *Love During the Time of the Cholera (El amor en los tiempos del colera)*. Mexico City: Diana.

Gelinas, D.J. (1983), The persisting negative effects of incest. *Psychiatry*, 46:312–332.

Greenberg, J.R., & Mitchell, S.A. (1983), *Object Relations in Psychoanalytic Theory*. Cambridge: Harvard University Press.

Grinberg, L. (1968), On acting-out and its role in the psychoanalytic process. *Internat. J. Psycho-Anal.*, 49:171–178.

——— (1985), Current concepts about the defensive processes (Conceptos actuales sobre los procesos defensivos). *Rev. de Psicoanalisis de Madrid*, 1:43–63.

Henderson, D.J. (1975), Incest. In: *Comprehensive Textbook of Psychiatry: Vol. 2*. 2nd ed., ed. Freeman, Kaplan, & Sadock. Baltimore: William & Wilkins, pp. 1530–1538.

Herman, J. & Hirschman, L. (1977), Father-daughter incest. *Signs: J. Women Culture Soc.*, 2:735–756.

——— Schatzow, E. (1983), Treatment of adult women with a history of incest. In: *Therapeutic Intervention in Father-Daughter Incest* (American Psychiatric Audio Review: Symposium of the 1982 American Psychiatric Association Annual Meeting). Washington, DC: American Psychiatric Press.

——— ——— (1984), Time-limited group therapy for women with a history of incest. *Internat. J. Group Psychother.*, 34:605–616.

Horowitz, M.J. (1976), *Stress Response Syndromes*. New York: Aronson.

Horwitz, L. (1983), Projective identification in diads and groups. *Internat. J. Group Psychother.*, 33:259–279.

——— (1984), The self in groups. *Internat. J. Group Psychother.*, 34:519–540.

Jacobson, E. (1964), *The Self and the Object World*. New York: International Universities Press.

——— (1971), *Depression*. New York: International Universities Press.

Jung, C.G. (1946), Psychology of transference. In: *The Collected Works of C.G. Jung: Vol. 16. The Practice of Psychotherapy*. London: Routledge & Kegan Paul, 1959, pp. 163–321.

Klein, M. (1932), *The Psycho-Analysis of Children*. London: Hogarth Press.

—— (1935), A contribution to the psycho-genesis of manic-depressive states. In: *Contributions to Psycho-Analysis*. London: Hogarth Press, 1948, pp. 262–290.

—— (1940), Mourning and its relationship to manic-depressive states. In: *Contributions to Psycho-Analysis*. London: Hogarth Press, 1948, pp. 311–338.

—— (1946), Notes on some schizoid mechanisms. *Internat. J. Psycho-Anal.*, 27:99–110.

—— (1952), Some theoretical considerations regarding the emotional life of the infant. In: *Developments in Psycho-Analysis*, ed. J. Riviere. London: Hogarth Press, pp. 198–236.

—— (1957), *Envy and Gratitude and Other Works, 1946–1963*. London: Tavistock.

—— (1961), *Narrative of a Child Analysis*. New York: Basic Books.

Knittle, B.J., & Tuana, S.J. (1980), Group therapy as primary treatment for adolescent victims of intrafamilial sexual abuse. *Clin. Soc. Work J.*, 8:236–242.

Kohut, H. (1968), The psychoanalytic treatment of narcissistic personality disorders: Outline of a systematic approach. *The Psychoanalytic Study of the Child*, 23:86–113.

—— (1971), *The Analysis of the Self: A Systematic Approach to the Psychoanalytic Treatment of Narcissistic Personality Disorders*. New York: International Universities Press.

—— (1977), *The Restoration of the Self*. New York: International Universities Press.

—— (1984), *How Does Analysis Cure?*, ed. A. Goldberg. Chicago: University of Chicago Press.

Kramer, S. (1983), Object-coercive doubling: A pathological defensive response to maternal incest. *J. Amer. Psychoanal. Assn.*, 31 (Suppl.):325–352.

Laplanche, J., & Pontalis, J.B. (1973), *The Language of Psychoanalysis*, trans. D. Nicholson-Smith. New York: Norton.

Levy, S. (1984), *Principles of Interpretation*. New York: Aronson.

Lystad, M.H. (1982), Sexual abuse in the home: A review of the literature. *Internat. J. Fam. Psychiat.*, 3:3–31.

McDonald, M. (1981), The psychoanalytic concept of the self. *Psychiat. Clin. N. Amer.*, 4:429–434.

Main, T.F. (1957), The ailment. *Brit. J. Med. Psychol.*, 30:129–145.

Marmor, J. (1972), Sexual acting-out in psychotherapy. *Amer. J. Psychoanal.*, 32:3–8.

Masson, J. (1982), *The Assault on Truth: Freud's Suppression of the Seduction Theory*. New York: Farrar, Straus & Giroux.

Ogden, T.H. (1979), On projective identification. *Internat. J. Psycho-Anal.*, 60:357–373.

Ormont, L.R. (1969), Acting in and the therapeutic contract in group psychoanalysis. *Internat. J. Group Psychother.*, 19:420–432.

O'Shaughnessy, E. (1983), Words and working through. *Internat. J. Psycho-Anal.*, 64:281–289.

Pines, M. (1982), Reflections on mirroring. *Group Analysis*, 15:2–26.

Poggi, R., & Ganzarain, R. (1983), Countertransference hate. *Bull. Menn. Clin.*, 47:15–35.

Putnam, F.W., Post, R.M., Guroff, J.J., et al. (1983), One hundred cases of multiple personality disorder. Presented at the Annual Meeting of the American Psychiatric Association. New Research Abstract #77, New York.

Rascovsky, M., & Rascovsky, A. (1950), On consummated incest. *Internat. J. Psycho-Anal.*, 31:144–149.

Redl, F. (1963), Psychoanalysis and group psychotherapy: A developmental point of view. *Amer. J. Orthopsychiat.*, 33:135–147.

Rizzuto, A.M., Peterson, R.K., & Reed, M. (1981), The pathological sense of the self in anorexia nervosa. *Psychiat. Clin. N. Amer.*, 4:471–488.

Russell, D. (1986), *The Secret Trauma: Incest in the Lives of Girls and Women.* New York: Basic Books.

Rutan, J.S., & Stone, W.N. (1984), *Psychodynamic Group Psychotherapy.* Lexington, MA: D.C. Heath.

Segal, H. (1974), *Introduction to the Work of Melanie Klein.* New York: Basic Books.

Stern, D.N. (1985), *The Interpersonal World of the Infant: A View from Psychoanalysis and Developmental Psychology.* New York: Basic Books.

Summitt, R. (1983), The child sexual abuse accommodation syndrome. *Child Abuse Neglect*, 7(2): 177–193.

Turquet, P.M. (1974), Threats to the personal identity in large groups (Menaces a l'identite personelle dans le group large). *Bull. de Psychologie*, special number:135–158.

Vander Mey, B.J., & Neff, R.L. (1982), Adult-child incest: A review of research and treatment. *Adolescence*, 17:717–735.

Wallerstein, R. (1985), Self psychology in practice. *Internat. J. Psycho-Anal.*, 66:391–404.

Winnicott, D.W. (1960), Ego distortion in terms of true and false self. In: *The Maturational Processes and the Facilitating Environment: Studies in the Theory of Emotional Development.* New York: International Universities Press, 1965, pp. 140–152.

Yalom, I. (1975), *The Theory and Practice of Group Psychotherapy.* New York: International Universities Press.

Zetzel, E. (1956), Current concepts of transference. *Internat. J. Psycho-Anal.*, 37:369–376.

Name Index

Subject Index